穿越紅色浪潮

——史明的中國革命歷程與台灣獨立之路

史明 著

陳序

　　1993年秋天史明先生翻牆回台，據悉是郭倍宏（美國北卡大學博士、台獨聯盟成員，稍早潛回台灣被捕入獄，出獄後參選台南市長）協助安排，當史明於10月30日準備在台南現身並參與郭倍宏的造勢活動，卻被台南當地的民進黨候選人以優勢的宣傳車、摩托車隊到機場演出搶人事件。當時我在自立早報（1993年11月1日）撰寫短論〈史明老先生的難題〉，一方面肯定他「此時提倡台灣民族論，不但可以作為抵抗中國的理論武器，並且可以揭露中國國民黨的外來政權本質，同時可以批判民進黨過早庸俗化的執政心態。老先生果然是運動家！」另一方面認為民進黨人可能對他的社會主義革命、台灣民族論不理解或不支持，卻以人際網絡包圍他，所以我斗膽警告「史老先生如何維護他自己的獨立自主，恐怕是推動其『獨立台灣』理想的首要條件。」

　　十六、七年過去了，歷經李登輝領導的本土化，以及民進黨轉型為選舉黨並兩度取得執政權，史明先生一直是獨立自主、乃至「孤獨地」宣揚他的台灣民族主義，給人一種「邊緣戰鬥」的印象。用史明自己提倡的現代革命四要素來看，理念、組織是有了，但是「計畫」——什麼是合乎台灣

大環境的戰略、戰術?「聯合(陣線)」——如何結合國民黨統治集團以外的各種力量?恐怕只有像民進黨這麼大的團體,才有條件談論這些。據我所知,九〇年代以來史明以他的獨台會做體制外的事,也許只有象徵意義,但他的思想卻是全方位的涵容體制內(選舉)、外(革命)路線,值得民進黨和本土社團參考、學習。

2009年年底史明在日本病倒了,返台就醫住在台北醫學大學附設醫院,逐漸好轉以後(2010年1月初)我有機會以四個下午的時間,在病房對他做口述歷史訪談,同時有機會接觸到照顧他的基層兄弟、仰慕他的青年學生以及北美洲台灣人教授協會(NATPA)的朋友,當時就決定為他辦一場「生命經驗分享會」。2010年3月14日這場會議終於得以在台北市羅斯福路的台大集思會議中心舉行,其間,台灣教授協會有幸擔負主要的庶務,至感光榮。

為了讓「史明生命經驗分享會」更為豐富,我們不但安排老中青齊聚一堂,且與史明的新書《穿越紅色浪潮》發表會共同舉行;從書中主文的中英對照以及NATPA前會長葉治平的介紹,都可以看到NATPA的影子,以及1980年代史明與北美的台灣留學生結下的深深情緣。如今這一段情緣終於可以在台北時空交會、再現,為台灣人的精神史留下一段佳話。同時,正逢台灣與中國關係日趨緊密/緊張的時刻,《穿越》一書應該可以發揮重要的警惕作用。是為序。

陳儀深 (台灣教授協會2009-2010會長)

自序

　　去年底（2009）在日本東京，突然罹患急性腎衰竭，一時曾昏迷不醒人事，但，在精神恍惚之中，自嘆一輩子為理想四處奔波勞累，人生的最終點站竟是在台灣海外結束，想起了在中國遭逢生活困難種種過往，更是心繫台灣，想說死也要死回台灣。

　　此次，慶幸有蔡丁貴、陳義丕、王獻極、Freddy等好友，特地急速趕至東京轉達台灣各界鄉親對我相當的關心，希望我的身體能早日康復，早日再回到台灣獨立革命的行列中。

　　一心想說絕對不能死在日本，在受到大家的關心及鼓勵之下，我也才能在重病危急之中身體漸漸康復，今日也才能在此和大家相見面。這次受到台灣教授協會（會長陳儀深）辦這麼隆重盛大鼓勵我的會，同時更將我過去的獨立思想的理論系統整理，出版這麼完整的書，重重地受到大家的照顧及鼓勵，實在從心裡感謝不盡，這是無法用言語來形容的，再深謝。

史明

2010初夏于新莊

速寫史明
A Sketch of Su Beng

作者：葉治平（Chih-Ping Yeh）
譯者： 陳清池（Ching-Chih Chen）

　　高挺的身材與一頭蓋頸的灰髮；粗布夾克與一件褪色的打鐵褲；塞滿書籍講義的旅行袋，和一捲講解台灣民族主義的掛圖；孜孜不倦地講述台灣革命的遠景；像是苦行的傳道者，卻是歷經風浪的革命家；在烽火連天的戰亂中驗證社會主義的理想，從反抗強權的鬥爭中體認台灣民族的自我。這是史明先生留給許多海外台灣人的印象，他一生傳奇的經歷與永不妥協的毅力，也一直吸引著熱情理想的青年學生。

Tall and with a headful of gray hair; a coarse jacket and a pair of faded blue jean; a rolled-up chart interpreting Taiwanese nationalism and a travel bag stuffed with books and lecture notes; tirelessly explaining his vision of Taiwanese revolution; seemingly a dedicated missionary, but really a life-long revolutionary; verifying the ideal of socialism through wars and finding Taiwanese national identity in his struggle against (imperialist) powers. This is the impression Mr. Su Beng has given overseas

Taiwanese. His story-like life-long experiences and his uncompromising will power have continuously attracted idealistic students.

史明，本名施朝暉，出身台北士林的大家族，童年在日本殖民政策的欺壓下成長，目睹台灣人遭受欺侮，而種下反對強權殖民的意識。1937年赴日，就讀政治科，並特別選擇研究帝國主義之殖民政策。由於當時主張殖民地解放者多為國際主義與社會主義國家，他也因此深受影響而走向社會主義革命的道路。

Su Beng's original name is Shih Chao-huei (Shi Diao-hui). He was born in an extended family in Shih-lin Distric of Taipei and grew up under the oppressive Japanese colonial rule. Having witnessed the suffering of Taiwanese from colonial suppression, he has come to possess anti-authoritarian consciousness. In 1937, he left for Japan to study political science by specifically focusing on colonialism of imperialist countries. Due to the fact that advocates of liberation from colonial rule were mostly from internationalist and socialist countries, Su was deeply influenced by them and followed the path of socialist revolution.

大學畢業後，史明抱著世界革命的理想，橫渡上海，投身抗日，並選擇加入傾向社會主義的中共部隊。他先被接到太行山一帶加入劉伯承的部隊（鄧小平是部隊政委），因深通

日語，受中共重視，所以受訓兩個月後，便被派到上海和北京之間從事敵後情報工作。他和一位女同志喬裝夫妻，爲了避免懷孕而妨礙工作，他自願接受「結紮」手術，因而一生無法生子育女。

Embracing the ideal of world revolution after his university graduation, Su sailed for Shanghai. In his decision to fight Japan, he chose to join the socialist-leaning Chinese Communist troops. He was first taken into Liu Bochen unit that was operating in Shansi Taihang mountain. (Deng Xiaoping was then the political officer of the unit.) Fluent in Japanese, he was highly regarded by the Chinese communists. Hence after a two-month training, he was dispatched to gather intelligence of the enemy operating between Shanghai and Beijing. He and a female comrade traveled as husband and wife. As pregnancy clearly would hinder their work, he voluntarily received male abortion surgery. That is why he has been unable to have his own children.

終戰後，史明被派到張家口的聯合大學再受訓練。1946年國共內戰開打，他再被派到西狼牙山一帶打游擊。在戰爭中，他看到被國民黨徵調來的台灣兵戰死很多，而被俘虜者又被中共軍隊送去當炮灰，心裡十分難過。因此向上級建議，應將台灣兵調到後方集中訓練，以待國民黨逃到台灣後善加利用。延安當局對此建議十分重視，於是將史明調到

晉冀魯豫邊區的軍政大學，負責組織「台灣隊」。八年的中
國經驗，已使他感受到台灣人和中國人在生活習慣，思想方
式與社會價值觀的差異，而逐漸萌生台灣意識。在軍政大學
這段時間裡，他又看到中共為了控制台灣兵，故意製造對立
來分化福佬人和客家人，更使他感覺到中共對付台灣人的手
段，與滿清及日本等外來殖民者並無不同，而終於體認出，
台灣與中國經四百年的長期隔絕，已形成兩個不同的民族。
中共是以統治異族的方法，來對待台灣人。

After the war, Su was sent to United University at
Zhangjiakou to receive further training. In 1946 the
civil war between the Nationalists and Communists
started. He was sent to Silangya mountain region to
fight guerrilla war. In battles, he saw many Taiwanese
soldiers died fighting for the Chinese Nationalist Party
that conscripted them. He was also greatly saddened
by Taiwanese who were captured by the Chinese
Communist troops but then sent out as cannon fodder.
He consequently proposed to his superior that the
Taiwanese soldiers should be sent to the rear to be
trained so that they could be properly employed when
the Nationalist Party fled to Taiwan. Having considered
his idea valuable, the authorities at Yenan sent Su
Beng to Military University, located at the border region
of several northwestern provinces, to take charge
of organizing a Taiwan Corps. During his 8 years
in China, Su came to see differences between the

Taiwanese and the Chinese in terms of their life habits, modes of thought and social values. He therefore gradually developed his Taiwanese consciousness. In addition, he saw the Chinese Communists' deliberately created division and rivalry between Holo Taiwanese and Hakka Taiwanese for the purpose of controlling Taiwanese soldiers. He felt the Communist tactics toward the Taiwanese was no different from that of Manchu and Japanese alien rulers of Taiwan. Finally, he realized that 400 years of separation between Taiwan and China had made them into two nations. The Chinese Communist were indeed using the way of ruling a different nation to deal with the Taiwanese.

在這期間，史明也親身經歷了中共慘無人道的土改政策。他看到地主被清算鬥爭後，遭百般凌虐而死；掃地出門的婦孺，因無人敢施捨救濟，而被活活餓死；清晨到井邊打水，也不時看到跳井自殺的屍體。這種情況與他理想中的社會主義完全不同，更使他對中共徹底絕望，而決心離開中國。1948年北京城投降，林彪與聶榮臻的部隊為搶先進城而打了起來。史明乘這混亂的機會，佯稱受派到台灣工作，以假路條從石家莊沿津浦線到濟南，又在當地農民的幫助下，沿麥田低處匍匐前進，躲過國民黨軍的機槍封鎖線，來到青島，然後向國民黨佯稱是台灣茶商而取得良民證，經過十分曲折的路程，終於在1949年5月回到台灣。

Meanwhile, Su had also personally witnessed the

brutality of Chinese Communist land reform. He saw landlords being struggled against and then killed after receiving various abuses. Driven out of their homes, women and children eventually starved to death when no one dared to help them. In the early morning, when fetching water from the well, he frequently saw corpses of people who had jumped into the well to commit suicide. The incompatibility of reality he had observed and his ideal of socialism contributed to his utmost disappointment with the Chinese Communists and his ultimate decision to leave China. In 1948 when the city of Beijing surrendered, two Communist troops, respectively led by Lin Biao and Nie Rongchen, actually battled for being the first to enter the city. Taking advantage of the chaos, Su cleverly claimed that he had been dispatched to work in Taiwan. With fake road permits, he traveled by train from Shijiazhuang to Jinan. And, with help from local peasants, he sneaked forward along wheat fields to avoid Nationalist Party troops' machine-gun-guarded line and eventually arrived in Qingdao. Disguising as Taiwanese tea merchant, he received a certificate of good citizenship from the Nationalist Party. After having overcome many difficulties, he finally returned to Taiwan in May 1949.

　　已經覺悟到台灣民族必須獨立的史明，看到二二八事件後的台灣社會，又萌生了武裝反抗的想法。他秘密組織了「台灣獨立武裝隊」，並收集到二十餘枝三八步槍，藏在

柑園中，準備伺機謀刺蔣介石。但行動被察覺，而遭通緝，逃亡數月後，他藏進一艘載香蕉輸日的輪船（天山丸），由基隆偷渡到神戶，但一上岸就被日本警察逮捕。日本政府原要將他以「偷渡犯」遣返台灣，史明自料返台必被國民黨酷刑至死，所以也偷藏一片刮鬍刀在衣角，準備一到台灣就割喉自殺。不料，國民黨把通緝史明的公文寄到日本，要求引渡，卻反而使日本官方認定史明為政治犯，而准許他居留並予以政治庇護。九死一生的史明，也因此開始他流亡海外長達四十一年的生涯。

Su, who had by then realized the need for Taiwan to become independent, saw the sad shape the post-228-massacre Taiwan society was in and came to entertain the idea of armed resistance. He secretly organized Taiwan Independence Armed Corps. Colleting and hiding more than twenty Model 38 rifles in an orange orchard, he waited for an opportunity to assassinate Chiang Kai-shek. Unfortunately his plot was discovered and he was forced to go hiding. After several months of hiding, he fled by stowing away in a Japanese freight ship carrying bananas from Chilong for export to Japan. When the ship arrived in Kobe, the Japanese police immediately arrested him. As the Japanese government was preparing to deport him back to Taiwan for illegal entry, Su knew that once arriving in Taiwan the Chinese Nationalist Party would torture him to death. He, therefore, hid a shaving razor in his sleeve for use to slice his throat once he landed in Taiwan. Unexpectedly, after having received from the Nationalist Government an official notice that demanded Japan to extradite Su, the Japanese government determined that Su had committed only political offense and consequently granted him political asylum. Having avoided certain death, Su began his exile overseas for the next 41 years.

　　爲了生活，史明在池袋開了一間「新珍味」小料理店，賣水餃和大滷麵。這期間，他在反省中，痛感台灣人對自己的歷史與社會發展疏於認識，而造成四百年始終不能擺脫殖民統治的慘境。所以一有時間，他就到日本國會圖書館或日比谷圖書館搜集有關台灣的歷史資料。同時他也重新檢討自大學時期就醉心信仰的社會主義，並一再苦思中共社會主義失敗的原因。他認爲，如果人類社會必須經過那種殘酷悲慘的過程，才能達到平等的理想世界，他寧願放棄追求理想。於是他潛心研究歷史，並重新學習馬克思思想。經過十年的沉潛苦思，他結論，中共的失敗是法西斯主義的失敗，而不是社會主義的失敗。

　　To make a living, Su opened at Ikebukuro District of Tokyo a small restaurant selling dumplings and noodle soup. During the 1950s, after long reflections, Su realized that due to failure to develop an understanding of their own history and society the Taiwanese for 400 years have not been able to escape from the misfortune of colonial rule. Thereafter, whenever he had time he would visit Japanese National Diet Library and Hibiya Library to gather materials on history of Taiwan. At the same time, he reevaluated socialism that he had come to believe in during his university years and pondered factors contributing to the failure of socialist system in Communist China. If human society has to go through the brutal and de-humanized process to reach an ideal egalitarian world, then he has decided that it is better to abandon the ideal. He subsequently devoted himself to the study of history and re-learned Marxism. After ten years of studious learning, he concluded that the failure of Communist China is the failure of fascism and not socialism.

　　1962年他出版了日文版的「台灣人四百年史」，1967年組織「獨立台灣會」，並出版「獨立台灣」月刊，開始從事島內台獨群眾運動。同時，他又以近二十年的時間，整理補充並以漢文撰寫翻譯，而於1980年出版了「台灣人四百年史」漢文版。他在序文中指出，這不是帝王將相的歷史，而是以勞苦人民的觀點，來記載台灣民族發展的過程。這是史明與其他歷史學者，在史觀上最大的不同之處。

　　In 1962, Su published his *400 Year History of the Taiwanese* in Japanese. In 1967, he organized Taiwan Independence Society, published Independent Taiwan monthly, and began in Taiwan mass movement for Taiwan independence. At the same time, he used nearly 20 years for further research and for the expansion of his book which he published in Chinese version in 1980.　In the book's preface, Su writes that the book is not a history about emperors, generals and high officials, but rather it is a record of the development of Taiwanese nation from the perspective of working classes.　It is this proletarian view of history that sets Su apart from other historians.

　　篤信馬克思思想的史明，對唯物史觀有眞灼的見解。他批判資本主義對人性的扭曲，但卻肯定資本主義在社會進化的歷史地位。他認爲，從落伍的封建社會，未經資本主義民主革命的洗禮，與社會主義階級革命的過程，就直接躍進人類道德觀念最終極的共產社會，是中共及一些共產國家失敗的主要原因。他反對列寧的獨裁，卻十分認同列寧的帝國主義論。所以他也一再強調，現階段的台灣革命，是殖民地解放的民族民主革命，而不是社會主義的階級革命，因此左派運動者應聯合進步右派和民族資本家，共同來推翻國民黨外來政權。這一觀點，與急進台獨左派非常不同。美麗島事件後，海外革命團體共同組成「台灣建國陣線」，台獨聯盟等右派團體堅持反對在陣線的宣言中加入「台灣民族」與「反帝」兩大綱領。史明先生爲了促進海外大團結，接受這個要求，但卻引起「台灣時代」等海外台獨左派對他全面的批判。

A faithful believer of Marxism, Su has a true

understanding of historical materialism. He critiques how capitalism has twisted human nature, but affirms the historical place of capitalism in the evolution of the society. He thinks that the failure of Communist China and other Communist countries is mainly due to an outdated feudal society's having jumped directly to mankind's ultimate moral goal of Communist society by skipping both liberal democratic revolution of capitalism and class revolution of socialism. He opposed the dictatorship of Lenin but agreed fully with his theory of imperialism. Therefore, Su has repeatedly stressed that the present stage of revolution in Taiwan is a nationalist democratic revolution of liberation from colonial rule and not a class revolution of socialism. The activists of the Left should unite with the progressive activists of the Right and national capitalists to overthrow the alien regime of the Nationalist Party. His view differs greatly from the Leftist faction of the Taiwan independence movement. After the Kaohsiung Formosan Incident (1979), the overseas revolutionary groups jointly formed the United Front for the Building of a Taiwan Country. The World United for Formosan Independence (WUFI) and other organizations on the Right were firmly opposed to any mention of "Taiwanese nation" and "anti-imperialism" in the United Front's Declaration. Su compromised so as to promote overseas Taiwanese cooperation, but he encountered an all-out criticism from the overseas Leftist groups such as "Taiwan Era (台灣時代)".

　　史明早期在日本曾加入台獨聯盟前身的「台灣青年獨立聯盟」，但因理念不同而離開（被開除）。在中產階級意識濃厚的海外革命陣營中，史明的確是與眾不同。他生活簡樸，毫無私慾，但對台獨運動卻十分慷慨。1981年美麗島週報發生財務危機，他傾囊相助，渡過難關。郭倍宏與李應元在北卡成立「台灣學生社」，他立即捐錢購買中文打字機，以出版學生運動刊物。他的料理店座落於東京池袋車站前的黃金地段，地產價值極高。為了出版「台灣人四百年史」，他將房產押出，但卻將台灣的版權無條件讓給鄭南榕先生。他的麵店生意鼎盛，但他也將收入全部投入台灣獨立運動。

Su had earlier joined in Japan the Taiwan Youth for Independence Alliance, a forerunner of WUFI. Due to ideological differences he was expelled from the Alliance. In the overseas revolutionary camp, that was full of middle class consciousness, Su was indeed different from the rest. He lived simply and devoid of selfish desires, but was generous with the cause of Taiwan independence movement. In 1981 when the Formosan Monthly experienced financial crisis, he provided all that was needed for the monthly to survive. When students leaders Kuo Pei-hong and Li Yin-yuan established "Taiwanese Students Society" in North Carolina, Su also donated necessary fund for the purchase of a Chinese type-writer so that they could publish student publications. Located at the prime location in front of Tokyo's Ikebukuro Train Station, the real estate value of Su's noodle soup restaurant is very high. For the purpose of publishing his book, he had used his real estate as collateral for a loan, but Su in turn unconditionally gave the book's copy right to Mr. Cheng Nan-jung. While the business of his noodle soup restaurant is good, Su has used the entire profit for Taiwan independence movement.

　　他為了接觸台灣群眾，常出資購買機票，招待一些工人，漁民或貧苦學生到日本「觀光」。料理店的三樓便是一間簡單的教室，許多台灣反對運動者，包括現在的政壇知名人物，都曾在那裡上過史明的「歷史課」。史明住在四樓，房間除了一蓆鋪在地板的棉被與一台老式的電扇，堆滿了書籍與資料。流亡海外的四十多年間，史明便是在那裡醞釀出台灣民族革命的理論。90年初我去日本探望他，看到他在料理店打烊後的深夜，又埋首趕寫新書「台灣民族革命與社會主義」，深感他不但是堅持理想的革命家，更是無私無我的奉獻者。他把台灣獨立運動當作畢生唯一的事業，了然一生，卻無怨無悔。我知道他想偷渡回台，勸他年事已高，何苦如此。他笑著回答，這是人生價值觀的問題。

　　In order to have close contacts with Taiwan masses, Su bought airplane tickets for many workers, fishermen and poor students so that they could visit Japan. The third floor of his restaurant is a simple classroom. Many Taiwanese opposed to the Chinese

Nationalist regime, including well-known politicians of
today, have attended Taiwan history class taught by Su
Beng.　Su himself lived on the fourth floor.　Aside from
an old-fashioned electric fan and a bed with comforter
in it, the room was stacked with books and other written
materials.　During his over-forty-year of exile, Su
was in that room developing his theory of Taiwanese
nationalist revolution.　In the early 1990s when I flied to
Japan to visit Su, I saw him, after closing his restaurant
in late evening hours, busily working on his new book
titled Taiwan Nationalist Revolution and Socialism.
He is a revolutionary who not only upholds his ideal
but also is a selfless contributor of his service and
financial resources.　He treats Taiwan independence
movement as his one and only life-time work.
Sacrificing his entire life, but he has no regret and no
complains.　I knew then he was planning to sneak back
to Taiwan, but why did he have to take such a risk at
such an advanced age?　He answered with a smile
that it is a question of one's view of life's meaning.

　　1993年11月，76歲的史明先生終於回到了睽違多年的台
灣，但被國民黨政府逮捕。在法庭上，他堅挺地站立，卻
側過頭去，不願正視法官，也拒絕答辯。有記者問他，是
不是「鮭魚返鄉」。他回答：「我回台灣的目的不是要回
家，而是要來推翻國民黨。」有些人笑他是「活在過去的唐
吉訶德」，但他不以為意。「To dream the impossible dream,
to fight the unbeatable foe」，正就是史明最吸引人的特質，

「To fight for the right, without question or pause」也是他一生的寫照。對史明而言，回到台灣，並不是流亡生涯的結束，而是台灣民族民主革命的另一啓端。

In November 1993, 76-year-old Su finally returned to Taiwan, but was immediately arrested by the Nationalist regime. In the court, he stood upright and resolutely. Unwilling to face the judge, he turned his head sideway and refused to answer any questions in his own defense. Responding to a reporter's question if he had returned home, he said, "I did not return to Taiwan to come home, but rather to overthrow the Nationalist Party." He did not mind some people's laughing at him for living like Don Quixote of the past. "To dream the impossible dream and to fight the unbeatable foe" is the most appealing characteristic of Su. And, "To fight for the right, without question or pause" is the portrait of his entire life. For Su Beng, returning to Taiwan is not the end of his exile life, but rather another beginning of Taiwan's national democratic revolution.

這些年來，每看到史明先生帶領「獨立台灣會」的車隊，擊鼓遊街，宣導台灣民族主義，總讓我聯想起那率領戰象隊，攀越過高山峭壁，擊潰羅馬兵團的歷史名將漢尼拔。但想到他90歲的高齡，仍挂著拐杖參加抗議示威及苦行，心中實在不忍。每次告訴他應多自保重，他總是回答：「能爲

台灣效勞，是我一生的光榮；現在還有力氣來繼續做點事，是我的幸運。」他堅信，民族解放是歷史的潮流，台灣民族獨立建國也一定會成功。所以，他將繼續堅定的走完這歷史所為他鋪下的人生道路。我們祈禱，史明先生早日康復。在往後的建國運動中，不論是否還能在看到他那「一頭蓋頸的灰髮，穿著粗布夾克與褪色打鐵褲」的身影，他的信念將永遠鼓舞我們繼續前進。

In the last few years, every time witnessing Su's leading a caravan of "Taiwan Independence Society" promoting Taiwanese nationalism while parading with drums' beating, I thought of famous General Hannibal's leading elephant army crossing mountain ranges to defeat Roman troops. However, I could hardly endure pains thinking of this over-90-year-old man walking with a cane to participate in protest demonstrations and walks. Whenever we asked him to take care, he always answered, "It is my honor to work for Taiwan. And, it is fortunate that I still have the energy to continue working." He firmly believes that national liberation is the trend in history and Taiwan will surely succeed in its independence and nation-building. He will therefore steadily continue to walk the road that history has laid for him. We pray for Su Beng's early recovery. In the future nation-building movement, his ideal and faith will forever sustain us to advance continuously whether or not we will still see the man "with a head of gray hair and clad in a coarse jacket and a pair of faded blue jean."

〔作者爲北美洲台灣人教授協會第二十三屆會長〕

第一部

紅色中國

1.
穿越紅色浪潮

一九四二年我決定早稻田大學畢業後，九月進入中國大陸，參加反帝抗日戰爭。我先在那年的四月到上海，進入新四軍解放地區參觀，後來才知道去的是江北的所謂「淮南黃花塘根據地」；六月回台，我和老祖母相辭時，當然沒讓她知道我要去中國參加抗日戰的事。

當時我是一個家人照顧得很好的青年人，在大學時代過著很自由、富裕，不必擔當什麼責任的學生生活，對外面的人心險惡，一點也無接觸，現在回想起來，可能我比起同年紀的青年人還相當幼稚。大學畢業後，我滿腦子馬克思的思想，自以爲加入中國共產黨的抗日隊伍，就可以把書本上的馬克思主義解放哲學，眞正的實踐起來。

馬克思主義的呼召

我在早稻田大學二、三年級時，很認眞研讀馬克思理論。他是以階級解放爲理論基礎，但是在第一國際的時期，尤其是馬克思、恩格斯，原本就很理解被抑壓民族之民族獨

立鬥爭的政治重要性。當時,第一國際所支持的主要民族鬥爭,是關於歐洲大陸的從屬民族解放革命(譬如波蘭、愛爾蘭及義大利)。馬克思對東方各個民族的革命,平常也積極在研究;他對中國的太平天國事件(1851-64),也有一定的認識,寫過「中國革命,是把火種投入產業組織的火藥庫,致使醞蓄很久的一般危機終於爆發,再引起其堅固結合的歐洲政治革命的爆發。」此外,馬克思在《資本論》即說到亞細亞各個殖民地解放的重要性。恩格斯在一八八三年也寫過對印度、波斯、埃及等殖民地革命的預測。

　　一九二〇年,第三國際第二屆大會在莫斯科召開,當時,列寧已成為世界勞動運動的偉大指導者,從世界各地參加的有三十五國、四十二支部代表。在大會上成立一連串的實踐上、政治上及組織上的方策,但是第二屆大會的最高政治問題,是列寧「有關民族‧殖民地問題的綱領」的決議案。列寧在這屆大會中的演講中,說到「與本國的無產革命一起,在殖民帝國的解體,能瓦解歐洲的資本主義體制」、「民族,有抑壓民族與被抑壓民族兩種類,地球上總人口的約七〇%是屬於被抑壓民族……,歐洲資本主義力量的主要泉源之一,是在殖民地的屬領與從屬國。資本主義列強若不廣泛的剝削掠奪殖民地,一時都不能存在。」

　　起初列寧的想法也是從歐洲出發,所以積極支援匈牙利、德國等國的勞動者革命。然而一九一九年匈牙利革命失敗,波蘭籍的羅莎盧森堡在德國成立的斯巴達克團(德國共產黨)也被打敗,盧森堡等革命者身亡,此時列寧才覺悟

到，要在資本主義強盛的歐洲革命成功，是非常不容易的，
應該把世界無產運動的中心放在資本主義勢力弱小的殖民
地，來支援殖民地革命運動。因此，第三國際乃開始把其無
產革命重點，灌注於對亞、非殖民地或從屬國「殖民地解放
・民族獨立」的支援工作，如一九二〇年朝鮮共產黨成立，
一九二一年中國共產黨成立，一九二二年日本共產黨成立，
一九二四年支援中國成立國共合作，在這種背景之下，謝雪
紅、林木順一九二六年去莫斯科受共產主義的訓練，回上海
後成立「日本共產黨台灣民族支部」（台灣共產黨，1928），
第三國際的策略，就是決定支持殖民地獨立，使資本帝國主
義垮台，促成世界的無產階級革命。

　　我在早稻田大學政治系的日本同學，都有服兵役的義
務，畢業後，他們都很堅定的要入伍當神風特攻隊的隊員，
為國家、為天皇與敵做生死戰，態度很悲壯，但也很值得
尊敬。相較之下，我雖然不用當兵，卻感覺心裡空虛。當時
在國際上，反殖民主義、民族解放運動風起雲湧，我左思右
想，竟然想到去中國從事「反帝鬥爭」的抗日戰，為民族
（台灣）、階級的解放奮鬥。這是我很突然、粗糙的想法，
卻是我決定要去中國共產黨解放區的純粹的動機。

　　因此，我去中國，不是因為漢族的情感，而是因為馬克
思主義反對日本帝國主義的立場。我根本沒考慮去重慶參加
蔣介石的國民黨軍，在我眼中，蔣介石是中國軍閥，國民黨
是土豪劣紳的封建殘餘集團，而且一直後退於中國大後方，
根本沒有與日本人打仗的意願。

無關中華民族問題

　　讀早稻田大學三年級時，我在一個偶然的機會，參加了
「馬克思理論讀書會」的秘密組織；我是高等學院同學大柴
滋夫介紹入會，他在二次大戰後，曾是日本社會黨的國會議
員。這個讀書會有七個日本學生，互相不知道各人的姓名、
學校等等，秘密的研習馬克思主義戰略戰術等等，其中，恰
好碰到一個中國的留學生，姓沈（假名），後來才知道他原
來是中國共產黨派來日本的地下工作人員，我才最後決定由
他引導，到中國共產黨在中國華北的解放區。

　　我很相信馬克思對民族問題的看法：「倘若階級問題解
決，民族問題也可以解決。」當時我與一般台灣人相同，知
道我們台灣人的祖先來自中國大陸，台灣人與中國人是同文
同種，但沒有「中華民族」的意識與感情。四百年來，台灣
和中國根本沒有往來，沒有社會關係，幾乎處於隔絕狀態；
清朝時期只有官僚、大商人能與中國大陸來往，在日本時
代，台灣一般民眾很少碰到中國人，也沒有去過中國大陸，
有去過中國廈門等地的人，在總人口說來，是一小撮人，大
部份是做走私的人及留學生。在廣大的中國，中國老百姓的
腦筋裡更是根本沒有「台灣」的意識，譬如，我一九四八年
在華北，碰到中國老百姓（農民大眾佔當時中國總人口的九成）
問我是哪裡人，我回答「台灣」，他們想了想後說：「那是
朝鮮的北面的地方吧（按：指日本）。」

　　我去中國和台灣與中國的民族問題完全無關。依照我當

時的人生觀，我只有兩個方向可以選擇，一是爲自己生活和
享樂打拚，一是爲社會、民族（台灣人）、階級等去奮鬥，
我最後選擇的是第二個方向。

　　我要離開日本赴中國參加抗日戰爭，固然是雄心勃勃、
熱情洋溢，可是對二十餘年來在日本生活圈的美好經驗、優
美的風景、精良的日本文化，以及朝夕共處的日本同學、
大學老師以及社會人的懷念等等（日本帝國統治台灣確實是殘
酷的殖民主義政策，但是日本人對台灣人的殖民優越感幾乎沒有，
在個人關係上是很友善的），有如風馳電掣的在腦海裡閃來閃
去，阿嬤的面容也突然浮現在我眼前，使我傷感唏噓，不能
自已。但我已置死生於度外，荊軻刺秦王的「風蕭蕭兮，易
水寒，壯士一去兮不復返！」在耳邊響起。

　　上車，趕路吧！

蘇州年代：我的第一份薪水

　　一九四二年九月，我沒有參加早稻田大學畢業典禮，倉
卒坐上火車，從東京到長崎換搭一萬噸的「長崎丸」。在火
車上或船要離開長崎時看到窗外景色，悲歡離合之情再度湧
上心頭。

　　坐長崎丸第二天早上起來，同船的日本人說：「快到
了。」我一看船邊，已從清澈的海水行駛到滂滂的河水，
才知道船已進入了長江的茫茫大海口，再走半天，船進入黃
浦江，最後看到蘇州河口的外白渡橋（garden bridge），以及

蘇州河岸邊的「百老匯大廈」（Broadway Mansion）。船再進入，其右邊是浦東，左邊是外灘，英國猶太人財閥沙遜擁有的高樓大廈，棟棟相連，林立於沿海路邊。船乃停泊在外灘靠岸。

到船上來接我的，是一個名叫朱斌（假名）的上海人，他馬上把我帶到蘇州，住進了一個「單間兒」。第二天，他帶我到一個警察派出所，領「戶口單」，這麼簡單的我就變成「中國人」，前後用過施明、林明、林煥等名字。由於我到上海或蘇州後，沒去日本領事館申報，所以自然的丟了日本戶口，等於放棄日本國籍了。

在蘇州住了十幾天，朱斌帶我去鎮江，過江到揚州，原準備帶我北上，走所謂第七師路線到「華北解放區」；江北一帶當時是「新四軍」解放區，司令員是陳毅。然而不知為何，徒步走了四、五天後又把我帶回蘇州。後來才知道蘇州有日本「登」部隊十三萬的許多中央機關，中共看我像個日本人，才把我調回替他們做地下情報工作，獲取日本軍事政治情報。

當時江南的政治局勢很複雜，原來孫文從事國民革命的左右手汪精衛，本是原南京政府的行政院長，一九三八年，他從重慶蔣介石政府管轄下的昆明逃到安南河內，發出投靠日本帝國主義的所謂「豔電」，於一九三九年三月，設立傀儡政權「中華民國國民政府」於日軍佔領下的南京，標榜「中日親善，共同反共」，與日本講和。至於蘇州，則是蔣介石軍統局降將丁默邨及李士群為了做所謂「清鄉工作」所

成立的江蘇省省都，當時前任省長是陳群（福建省福州人），後任是任援道（江蘇省宜興人）。

一九四二年至一九四五年，我在蘇州的那段時間，是由江蘇省教育廳長袁殊（其實是中共地下幹部），介紹我去位於名園「拙政園」（明正德年間，御史王獻臣建立）的省政府經濟科上班，但我不必工作，每星期只去辦公室報到一次，就可以領到薪水。這是我頭一次拿到的薪水，也才知道什麼叫做「坐領乾薪」。雖然已經正式上班，我連北京話或蘇州話都不會講，起先是用寫字或手比，那時起開始學ㄅㄆㄇㄈ，台灣話和北京話是同文同種，學起來較容易懂，不過我算是很用功在學，譬如每天走在街上，沿途就唸唸招牌上的字學北京語，但蘇州話我至今還搞不清楚。我常到蘇州熱鬧地區的館前街後面，吃有名小吃八寶飯及粽子等。

當時旅居華中一帶的台灣人不多，較有名氣的有二林蔗農反日事件的領導者李應章，改名「李偉光」，在上海擔任中共的聯絡人；以及台北和尚州（蘆洲）人李友邦，他統領幾十個台灣義勇軍，在浙江省金華做蔣介石國民黨軍（第四戰區，司令顧祝同，國民黨上海地下工作領導蔣伯誠）和日本軍交易的經紀人；此外，藍國城在南京做汪精衛偽政府軍總參謀長；王伯榮、林坤章在上海開振亞銀行；其他如楊肇嘉、楊白成枝等抗日份子，也在上海法租界。

一九四三年夏天，我曾赴廈門一趟省親。待了半個月後，廈門組織叫我帶中國女性「阿雲」和叫著陳武的男人一起回上海，在上海和阿雲裝成夫婦同居於蘇州北寺塔附近，

因怕懷孕而妨害日後的革命工作，我就不管三七二十一，也沒想我要傳施家後代，在上海北四川路的一家日本人醫院，毅然地就結紮絕後。

我的小弟林朝陽，因有逃兵意圖，也來到上海，後來去日本軍南京部隊報到入伍，所以常到蘇州找我。吳克泰（後來做中共地區台灣民主自治同盟常務理事，本名詹世平，宜蘭人，和朝陽在台北二中同班，他在台北高等學校時，志願當日本兵，被派到上海「登」部隊司令部擔任翻譯官，據說常看到日軍殺國民黨地下人員的悲慘場面），也屢次到蘇州我家過夜。

蒐集情報的奢靡歲月

據聞，中共黨中央曾在一九三八年設立「東南局」，書記項英（湖北省武漢市人，新四軍副軍長，皖南事變時戰死），負責江蘇、浙江、安徽、江西等長江下游國民黨地區秘密地下工作。一九四一年「皖南事變」後，東南局改為周恩來、董必武領導的「東方局」，當時八路軍在上海的地下工作，全由潘漢年及方方、李克農等人負責。

潘漢年是江蘇省宜興人，早時在郭沫若、成仿吾的「創造社」主編《洪水》，後來在中共黨中央直屬文化工作委員會任第一書記、華中局聯絡部長，抗日戰爭前後在上海、香港從事地下黨秘密工作，廣泛和所謂反蔣反共的「第三黨」，沈鈞儒、鄒韜奮、宋慶齡、史良、黃炎培、馬敘倫、沙千里、張瀾、章乃器、章伯鈞及作家郭沫若、老舍、田

漢、茅盾等做抗日救亡工作。解放戰爭後期，他以「新政治協商會議」為號召，使三百五十餘人所謂「開明紳士」安全到達解放區，繼之當中共上海市副市長。然在一九五五年他以「內奸」罪嫌被逮捕審查，一九八二年死後才恢復名譽。

我在蘇州時，從中共地下人員，零零碎碎聽到很多情報。日本佔領軍「登」部隊的特務機關也在蘇州，經過中共地下人員層層牽線，我遂認識了特務機關長田島貫一（假名松井），由我接近套取情報，所以我與日本特務頻繁往來於蘇州、上海、南京等地，同時與地下人員藍田、李戢等人一起在上海大世界對面的弄堂裡借民房為「地下聯絡站」，與日本軍人喝酒、跳舞、嫖妓，天天花天酒地，生活日趨糜爛。

日本海軍在上海有「武官府」小笠原大佐，是我父親的友人，江陰有「陸戰隊」隊長有働，是我早稻田大學的後輩，他們都是我獲取情報的來源，還能聽取陳寶川從日本秘密情報單位所得來的情報，所以有關日軍情報的搜集頗有斬獲。

此時我認識了一個台灣艋舺人陳寶川，他從滿洲國法政學院畢業後，被派來蘇州，在松井底下做情報工作；這個學院是專門用來培養偽滿洲政府的官僚，台灣人很多到這個學校就讀。陳對人姿勢很低，很虛偽，他所稱的經歷大多與事實不符，但是他的太太很懂得人情世故。日本戰敗後，他對從重慶來接收日本特務機關的戴笠軍統人員逢迎，立即受軍統提拔，被派回台灣做特務工作並在台灣大學做訓導工作，

同時以調查局等特務黑網爲背景，早期當國大代表，後來在蔡萬春國泰系統的國華人壽做過董事長，台灣合會儲蓄公司董事長，第一銀行董事長，彰化銀行董事長等，最後在陳立夫中統系的交通銀行（中國四大銀行之一）擔任常務董事，也是蔣經國親生子章孝慈的義父，可見他在特務黑網裡是一步登天，地位很高。

後來一九四九年回台時，陳寶川介紹蔣經國在蘇聯時的同學高理文（素文）給我認識。高理文在贛南時代是替蔣經國辦報紙，蔣在上海打老虎時亦替蔣經國抓孔祥熙的兒子（隨即被蔣經國釋放）。他在台灣是中央信託局最高顧問，但他卻仇恨蔣家四大家族（蔣、孔、宋、陳）的無法無天，反對蔣父子的法西斯特務政治，遂遭特務監視與跟蹤，後來移民美國。

蘇州在春秋時代是屬吳國之地，隋唐時代開闢運河，商業、手工業發達，名勝古跡、寺塔名園尤其多，譬如北寺塔、獅子林、寒山寺、虎丘等，東有長江、西有太湖，馬可波羅在《東遊記》中，也描寫蘇州「是一個壯麗的大城，居民有巨量的生絲，不僅製成綢緞，使所有人都穿上絲綢，還足以運銷到其他市場。」蘇州的寒山寺內則有張繼的〈楓橋夜泊〉石碑：

月落烏啼霜滿天
江楓漁火對愁眠
姑蘇城外寒山寺

夜半鐘聲到客船

上海，所謂「萬國殖民地」的中心都市，分爲法租界、日本租界及共同租界，這個治外法權的大都市，是完全洋溢著西洋人氣氛的世界級大港口，外國船隻頻繁進出，重工業、商業發達，上海市的中國人很多是外商買辦（葡萄牙語 comprador），生活奢侈虛榮，輕快但輕浮。當時在上海流行著「天堂歌」：「上海呀本來呀是天堂／只有歡樂沒有悲傷／住了大洋房／白天又麻將／晚間跳舞場／……財神爺竟跟他們通了商／洋錢鈔票總也用不光／出入呀／汽車呀／樂洋洋。」但當時在法租界公園入口，還掛著「狗和支那人不許進入」的牌子。上海郊外有國民黨的「忠義救國軍」（軍統特務周偉龍、馬志超、毛森輪流任總指揮）。

我每往上海，最喜歡的是去聽京戲。海派麒麟童唱「蕭何月下追韓信」，四小旦之一的張君秋唱「甘露寺」，尤其是演關公名角林樹森演「華容道」，我都喜歡去聽。我一面聽戲，一面想起跟母親去大稻埕後車頭的新舞台看京戲的往事，我已成爲標準「戲迷」了。另外在法租界，有外國人經營的「蘭心大戲院」，所演出俄羅斯作曲家史特勞汶斯基的「火鳥」芭蕾舞蹈，也很樂了我的耳朵和眼睛。

但是，我在上海時，卻發生一件令我意想不到的事件。

有一天，我在法租界與共同租界的交界，熱鬧的南京大街上走著，一時沒注意去踩到一個中國人的腳，當然如同在台灣及日本一般，隨即向他道歉，想不到那個人迅雷不

及掩耳的躍站起來，隨即捉住我的領帶，同時以上海話向我大聲吼叫，我聽不懂上海話，好似是在指摘我爲何踩到他的腳。罵得挺厲害，我只有以日本語的 "すみません"（對不起），向他連聲道歉。然另一個晴天霹靂的事，周圍的路人很快就將我們層層包圍，而在一旁看熱鬧，我只有小心道歉，這樣也鬧了將近一個小時，我從來也沒遇過這種窘況，突然靈光一閃，也許以錢就能解決，我就將口袋裡的錢包拿出來，他卻馬上拿了錢後，就好似沒事發生般轉身就離開現場，而一旁的人群也隨即散開離去。我百思不得其解的回到我上海的住處，將剛發生的事情一五一十的告訴同宿的友人。更令我驚訝得說不出話來的是，他給我的回答竟然說這是我的不對，他跟我說：你向他道歉這就是你的不對，你應該說：臭你媽的，爲什麼把腳伸得那麼長，害我去踩到，走，走，走……？我一聽到同宿的話，就感到混身不對勁，爲什麼是這樣呢？

　　在上海時，我穿香港衫及西裝，上海人也穿香港衫及西裝，我也沒覺得有什麼不一樣的地方，市街也跟大都市一般，然而經過這樣的事件，才讓我頭一次深切感受到中國人和台灣人是這麼的不同。

毛澤東主義在張家口

　　一九四五年十一月，中共上海地下組織叫我到北京取鴉片。當時中共在華北、蒙疆一帶種植鴉片，運到天津、上

海等處，由天津、上海再轉運別處出售，做爲地下工作的重要資金來源。早在一九三六年，日本爲了侵略中國，先從滿洲國攻打內蒙古爲前哨戰，趕走綏遠軍閥傅作儀軍團，並使蒙古德王和漢人李守信成立了「蒙疆政府」，繼之一九三七年發生中日事變，日本敗戰後，中共接收蒙疆政府爲「晉察冀邊區政府」，同時也把該區鴉片的種植、製造及銷售一起接收，設立「戒煙局」控制鴉片事業。在日本軍佔領華北地區（樹立「華北政務委員會」，委員長王克敏）的時候，中共都是利用津浦、京漢兩大鐵路幹線，以及天津到上海的海路，利用日本軍人替他們運鴉片，流散於國民黨地區及東南亞地區。

當日本在一九四五年八月十五日戰敗之際，中共爲了防止美式武裝的國民黨軍過江北上佔領華北，即把這兩條鐵路幹線，在一夕之間拆光，使南北交通完全斷絕。因無法用鐵路來運送鴉片，共黨才叫我去北方設站做輸送鴉片的工作。先前我父親在廈門當公賣局長時，我是那麼激烈反對他染上毒癮，如今回想起來，當年一定是被「革命」兩字沖昏了頭，像吃了「符仔」一樣，才如此唯唯諾諾做出不可思議的事情。

一九四五年九月，蔣介石派來的廣西派巨頭李宗仁爲司令官，佔領北京。派我去拿鴉片的是晉察冀軍區城工部的人，給我鴉片的是晉冀魯豫軍區的人；我到北京接到鴉片後，本來要立刻轉給下一手帶去上海，不知爲何失聯了，所以一直在北京等到翌年一九四六年二月，才和晉冀魯豫的地

下人員（瞿、白兩人）聯絡上。

　　北京是中國將近一千年來的政治文化中心，有故宮、景山、中南海、頤和園、天壇等名勝古跡，尤其是故宮的紅磚綠瓦，被認爲世界罕見的人間奇景。但是我對於北京所好，不是別的，是故都唯有的「京戲」。我在北京三、四個月中，幾乎都集中於聽戲這件事，在四大名旦之中，程硯秋的「武家坡」、尚小雲「三娘教子」、荀慧生「玉堂春」、老生的譚富英「捉放曹」、馬連良「借東風」及大花臉金少山「霸王別姬」等等，我都聽得好過癮。「父女們打漁在河下／家貧那怕人笑咱／桂英兒掌穩啊舵／可憐我年邁蒼蒼氣力不佳……」（打漁殺家）

　　一九三六年六月，寫過《紅星下的中國》一書的史諾（Edgar Snow），到延安見毛澤東，毛澤東在談話中，同意朝鮮及台灣的獨立。同年五月，第三國際宣佈解散。一九四五年四月，中國共產黨召開第七次黨員代表大會，在劉少奇（文化大革命時，被毛澤東鬥爭橫死）等人安排之下，毛澤東終於當選黨主席，集黨政軍大權於一身，從此開始了毛澤東的個人獨裁。當時，「中國共產黨中央軍事委員會」是共黨軍事最高機構（黨總書記兼任主席），主席毛澤東，副主席朱德、周恩來，副主席兼總政治部主任劉少奇，副主席兼總參謀長葉劍英，八路軍總司令朱德、副總司令彭德懷、參謀長葉劍英。

　　涉世未深，單純且有傻氣的我，一下子跨出一大步，與過去的舊生活一刀兩斷，闖進朔北寒冷的新生活，投入驚濤

駭浪，去翻騰、去隨波逐流，此後我的假名為林鐸。

　　總之，一九四五年十一月，我在晉冀魯豫軍區地下人員介紹下，從上海龍華機場搭乘美國水上機到青島後，再坐上中華航空的飛機，抵達北京。一九四六年三月，從北京搭乘國民黨軍控制下往張家口的平綏鐵路，在康庄下車，經由當時中立地帶的居庸關，換搭馬車到達共軍解放區晉察冀（山西、察哈爾、河北三省）軍區，當時該區司令員兼政治委員是聶榮臻，副司令員蕭克，城工部長劉仁（後來當北京副市長，文化大革命時，被紅衛兵整死）。

　　我和在北京交識的日本女朋友（日本大使館職員）平賀協子，一起到達晉察冀軍區「中央局」（書記兼司令員及政治委員聶榮臻、彭真、劉仁等人）所在地的張家口。我對張家口市的頭一個印象，就是到處都貼上「中國共產黨萬歲」、「毛澤東三大政策」（根據地、土地改革、游擊戰）、「背槍上前線、荷鋤至田庄」等標語或壁報。我們就住在招待所，但是立即被禁止自由行動，處處都有小鬼監視，真是晴天霹靂，實在是豈有此理，而且生活不同，不自由得令我訝異。

　　到一九四六年四月，我和平賀被帶到聯合大學（校長成仿吾），進入補習班學習。那個時候，有很多在延安「魯迅藝術學院」（魯迅在生前時被罵是帝國主義爪牙，死後卻被稱為文化愛國者）教書的文化人，被派來聯合大學教書，如丁玲（著名女作家）、蕭軍（魯迅的高足）、蕭三（留蘇著名詩人，共黨高級幹部）、艾青（著名詩人）等人。因為當時我是唯一從台灣自願來的台灣人，其他有三個台灣人都是做日軍被俘

虜的，所以他們都很珍惜我，常找我談話。

　　聯合大學有很多從國民黨地區或淪陷區來的青年學生，學生都十來個爲一班，合宿共寢，天天吃小米飯，配豆腐白菜湯。我因水土不服吃不習慣，身體一天天差，亦有久年的出血性痔瘡，因爲便所都沒有門，也沒有隔牆，有一次，蹲茅廁時被同學見到出血得厲害，丁玲、蕭軍等聽到了就常來看我，並領我去教員餐廳吃好飯。這些人都有些人道主義的色彩，可是共黨把人道主義當做一種資產階級思想，甚至是反革命的，這點是我到解放區後頭一次碰到的難關。一九四一年在延安時，丁玲、蕭軍因曾被毛澤東進行公開批判，透過「文藝談話」或「整風運動」，肅清他們的知識份子、小資產階級思想，後來被流放於東北地方。

　　聯合大學時代，以班爲單位，天天看毛澤東的〈新民主主義〉（1940）與〈論聯合政府〉（1945），列寧〈國家與革命〉（1917），以及看《解放日報》。白天開會討論，晚上做自我檢討或寫自傳，有時全校學生一千多人集合聽講「唯物史觀」，但是我覺得講師的理論基礎比日本大學差得太多。像說美國擁有原子彈是反動的，蘇聯若有原子彈則是革命等的言論，我聽到後覺得實在很不可思議。又譬如說，馬克思本身是以恢復在資本主義體制喪失的「人性」爲出發點，是解放的思想，然而自從我們到解放區以來，時時刻刻受到監視，有機會出校外時，也必須班長或扛槍的小鬼帶著走。這給我帶來不少的疑惑。（這就是毛澤東個人獨裁的產物，根本就悖離社會主義的原則。）

游擊戰的初體驗

抗日時期，長江以南的國民黨地區，有很多年輕學生受到蔣介石「百萬青年百萬軍」的號召，起而抗戰；然而跟日軍打仗的，都是長江以北的中共游擊隊，國民黨軍幾乎和日軍沒打過多少仗。日本敗戰後，蔣介石政府立即從重慶返都南京，軍人、官僚等都紛紛奔走淪陷區，去接收或掠奪日本軍民留下的龐大設施或財物，納為己有。這時，一大群青年學生軍人被棄如敝屣，其中許多人既被迫退伍，又無法歸鄉，他們聽到共黨號召：「解放區是有飯大家吃，有活兒一起做，就職上學，都很自由」，便信以為真，從西安或北京、天津等地奔赴解放區者，比比皆是。我在聯合大學碰到不少這種人。

國共和談談判的所謂「三人小組」（美國的馬歇爾將軍、張群、周恩來）談判破裂，一九四六年七月「國共內戰」打起來，駐東北的美式裝備國民黨軍集中十幾個師，兵分東西兩路，企圖佔領張家口，擬打通平綏鐵路，割斷華北與東北的聯絡線。共軍第一二九師（陳再道指揮）在地方武裝部隊配合下，掩護晉察冀中央局等政府機關撤出張家口，轉往阜平。我們所屬的蒙疆銀行在撤退的過程中，由於碰到從東北南下的國民黨軍前哨部隊，這些中共政府機關的後續部隊便繞過宣化、涿鹿、岔道、蔚縣，再繞到易縣、狼牙山等地，邊行軍邊打仗，我就是在這三個月間，頭一次參加游擊戰，才先到了山西省北部的靈丘。

　　在靈丘暫時停軍時，我經過思索，向上級提出要求讓我學「軍事」。組織上竟然派我往應縣，進入「步兵幹部學校」。該校是從前線調下營級幹部，專為施予再教育訓練的晉察冀軍區最高軍事學校。他們軍人學生都有很多戰鬥經驗，但都是從農村被徵兵出來，幾乎不識字，文化水準低，倒也敦厚樸實，我入學後和他們一起學習了游擊戰術和毛澤東思想、紀律、帶兵等，和他們搞得還不錯，有時聽他們講起得意洋洋的戰場經驗，也會感到興奮。

　　在步兵幹部學校三個月受訓後，我就被調回「晉察冀蒙疆銀行」資料室做調查工作，也做驢子運送隊的保送工作。在行軍當中，我們部隊和聯合大學團隊，若即若離的一起行軍，和從國民黨區來的聯大學生，常有接觸或共住一個村莊的機會，在行軍中，恰逢各鄉村正在搞土地改革與反國民黨的「人民裁判」。

　　一九四六年延安共黨中央發出所謂「五四指示」「反國特」，命令各鄉村進行土地改革與殲滅國民黨員，企圖使中國由封建社會轉型為共產主義社會，然而共黨不僅取走地主的田產，還消滅他們的生命，有的被活活打死，有的被凌遲至死，連其家屬也無一倖免。這段整風，遂暴露出中共獨裁醜惡的本質。此時，共黨把農民大眾分為地主、重農、中農、貧農四個階級，即以地主和重農為鬥爭對象，從黨中央派遣「管監團」在各村鄉做督促和監視。他們用極其殘忍的手段，消滅地主重農與國民黨員的生命，且流放其家屬；這些家屬被強制掛上某地主眷屬的牌子，趕出家鄉，其他村莊

不敢予以收容，任令他們倒地餓死路旁。中共黨員口裡常掛著一句「罪及九族」，此時才深深體認到這句話的實在。

　　然而，剛從國民黨地區進入中共解放區的學生，因大多是地主、資本家或中小工商業者家庭出身，先前在聯合大學的時候，就受到要不斷檢討的強制壓迫，差不多都已垂頭喪氣，再看到在人民裁判時地主與國民黨員遭極嚴格的流血鬥爭，在恐懼、苦惱之餘，不少人都受不了衝擊，開始逃跑。但是中共的組織與行政是密集的、嚴厲的，無論任何工作人員，移動時都要攜帶各單位所發給的路條，沒帶路條的逃亡者，一定遭鄰村黨支部的民兵抓回來。他們晚上逃跑後，翌日早上就被送回原地的鄉村，被共黨幹部打得死去活來，於是有人第二次、第三次逃跑……，熬不過的就跳古井了。

　　我親眼目睹這樣的慘事，尤其二、三天前我才還和他講過話的中國青年朋友，有天一早大家在古井漱口洗臉時，舀水的勺子放不下去取水，撈上來的就是這個青年人，一個撈完，又撈上來一個，死屍都是身體前彎的。我見到這樣的慘狀，對中共大失所望，所受的衝擊很大，可以說是驚慌失措，連飯也吃不下。

　　我只有胡思亂想，想來想去，想到在聯大所聽到的講課，或許我已吃多了「剝削飯」，這樣吃苦是一種報應，這樣熬過了，才猛然驚醒：「我不是中國人，還有一條生路，死也要回台灣死才是。」此時，我歸台的心念開始萌芽。

流行歌還得偷偷唱

我們將撤出張家口時，我是在蒙疆銀行資料室工作，這對我的情緒是不小的打擊，因為我到解放區來的目的是要搞「革命」，為什麼得做這種普通業務的工作呢？此時，一個黨組織幹部對我說：「革命要你做什麼，你都得去做，無論掃地皮，清水溝……」，我才稍微懂得什麼是具體的革命工作。在撤出張家口的行軍中，我成為銀行的掩護部隊一員，跟押著兩百多隻騾子隊的陳隊長，輸送銀行的黃金、龍銀等儲備金及一些文書檔案，向阜平出發。在途中屢屢遇到國民黨軍的前哨部隊，使我充分嚐到所謂「游擊戰」的臨危滋味，有時雙方同時佔據一個村的東西兩角，天色一暗，槍聲就搭搭搭……互響起來，有時突然遭遇敵軍，就地挖地道，靠近敵人聲東擊西，大打一仗。

共軍經過村莊時，叫老百姓騰空民房讓大家住下。駐在村莊的晚上，上級就動員士兵看批鬥吊打的地主重農或國民黨員，或參加人民裁判公審，叫你學學「貧農對地主的階級仇恨」。但一路走來，大家暗地裡對上級也會心生不滿，因上級對成員採取差別待遇，特別照顧黨員，輕視非黨員，黨員生病馬上看醫生，但非黨員生病了頂多分幾個雞蛋，叫你多睡覺。

從國民黨地區來的新學生，連唱歌都受干涉，要唱自己喜歡的歌時得低聲偷唱，一不小心就受批判。一九三〇年代駐上海的共黨文化工作代表周揚（後來的中央黨部宣傳部

長），提出所謂「國防文學」，專爲攻擊魯迅等民主作家的作品，巴金的《家》《春》《秋》等反封建文藝作品，在解放區也屬禁書。來自華中、華南的青年人，都喜歡唱當時流行的歌曲，如王人美的「漁光曲」、周璇的「送君」、龔秋霞的「秋水伊人」等等。他們特別喜歡唱曹禺作詞、洗星海作曲的「夜半歌聲」，但這條反封建的民主歌曲，因曹禺是受共黨批判的戲劇家，他們也得偷偷唱。我很喜歡這條民主歌謠，也學到並跟他們低聲唱。

夜半歌聲

空庭飛著流螢，高台走著狸貓，人兒伴著孤燈。
梆兒敲著三更，風淒淒，雨淋淋，花亂落，葉飄零。
在這漫漫的黑夜裡，誰同我等待著天明？
誰同我等待著天明？

我形兒是鬼似的猙獰，心兒是鐵似的堅貞，
我只要一息尚存，誓和那封建的魔王抗爭！
啊！姑娘，只有你的眼，能看破我的生平，
只有你的心，能理解我的衷情。
你是天上的月，我是那月邊的寒星，
你是山上的樹，我是那樹上的枯藤，
你是池中的水，我是那水上的浮萍。

不，姑娘，我願意永做墳墓裡的人，

埋掉世上的浮名，

我願意學那刑餘的史臣，盡寫出人間的不平。

哦，姑娘啊！天昏昏，地冥冥，

用什麼來表我的憤怒，唯有那江濤的奔騰，

用什麼來慰你的寂寞，唯有這夜半歌聲，

唯有這夜半歌聲。

　　我記得共黨公開唱的是：「跨過祖國的千水萬山／衝過敵人的封鎖線……」、「東方紅／太陽昇／中國出了一個毛澤東／他是中國的大救星／呵啦嘿呀」。至於舞蹈、戲劇，就是天天「扭秧歌」（西北地方的民俗舞蹈），及由軍文工隊、村文工隊、農會文工隊等在早晝夜連續演「白毛女」。共黨把同一件事重複不斷的方式，使大家厭煩還不肯罷休，大家雖心裡覺得厭煩不耐，但表面上卻得假裝拍手叫好。開會時也同樣，中央局大幹部一定要一件事重複演講，如周揚（中央局宣傳部長）、成仿吾（聯合大學校長）等，他們的口音都帶著相當濃厚的方言，很難聽懂演講的內容，得到隔天看《解放日報》，才能了解他們在講什麼。

建議組成台灣隊

　　話說一九四五年，蔣家國民黨佔領台灣後，在台灣新竹、苗栗、嘉義、台東等地抓「台灣兵」，為數一萬餘人，編成「新編七十師」，師長是陳頤鼎（中將，東北人，黃埔三

期畢業）。一九四六年底，蔣介石把新編七十師調派於黃河沿邊（山東省西南地區）去打內戰，初戰就在徐州大敗戰，幾乎潰不成軍。而在一九四七年五月，中共八路軍，改稱「人民解放軍」，同年六月三十日晚，劉伯承、鄧小平領導的「南下大隊」十三萬，自山東省臨縣至張秋鎮三百餘里地段，強渡黃河，劉鄧大隊以晉冀魯豫野戰軍第七十縱隊在魚台、金鄉、羊山、巨野、豐縣、曹縣一帶，發動「魯西戰役」，國民黨被打得一敗塗地，「七十軍」（前新編七十師改編的，軍長高吉人）被打垮，台灣兵近一萬皆被俘虜。

一九四八年六月，國民黨軍八十萬、人民解放軍六十萬在徐州以東大會戰，國民黨軍一一被攻破，每次俘虜五萬、十萬人，黃百韜兵團盡遭殲滅。又在一九四八年十一月的「淮海戰役」、「徐蚌會戰」中，蔣介石國民黨軍大兵團幾乎被殲俘，黃維兵團遭殲滅，副總司令杜聿明被俘虜，唯獨機械兵團司令邱清泉敵前自殺。故在一九四六年六月初戰時蔣介石聲明：「八小時內消滅中原人民解放軍，兩個星期內佔領蘇北，三個月到六個月內擊潰人民解放軍主力」的作戰計畫，全化為烏有。

一萬多名台灣兵被劉鄧大軍俘虜後，因台灣囝仔都受過日本軍事訓練，所以中共令其脫下國民黨軍服，換上中共的軍服，又被派往前線去與國民黨軍對峙，台灣兵驍勇善戰，強硬直衝，因而傷亡慘重。

我在《解放日報》得知台灣兵每次都二、三百名一批一批陣亡，很心痛，今天打共軍被俘，明天打國民黨軍犧

牲陣亡，世上哪有這樣悲慘的事。此時的我，更痛恨外來統治的罪惡，左思右想之後，才想藉由當時局勢的演變，提起台灣兵的事於上級讓共黨知道，也許對台灣兵有幫助，所以貿然向陸軍幹部學校政治部主任吳西（做人忠誠老實的老共產黨員，廣西人）提議：「人民解放軍進攻國民黨地區勢如破竹，短日子必能征霸全中國，不久將來蔣介石難免逃亡台灣，所以，不要使近萬的台灣兵在前線消耗殆盡，必須調到後方施以政治訓練，讓他們返台後做革命工作，對革命才有利。」

吳西等學校的幹部們，對我突然的時局的預測，誠是吃了一驚的樣子，一定是馬上向延安報告。在延安的黨中央，不到一個月的時間，就來電要調我從阜平（晉察冀軍區中央所在地）往晉冀魯（山東）豫（河南），該軍區司令員是劉伯承，政治委員鄧小平。一九四七年三月八日，我在阜平中央局招待所，看到報導台灣二二八大革命爆發的《解放日報》，心裡頗感波動，然而中國共產黨始終偽造歷史，譬如在一九七五年，廖承志還硬說：「二二八大革命是毛澤東及其中國共產黨領導的中國革命的一部份。」

一九四七年三月，我和平賀兩人，每人身背著兩華斤半的棉被和日常用品共五、六華斤，由一個小鬼監視同行，走了四十餘天，經過平關、黨城、曲陽、定縣、高邑等地，從邢台轉西，經過武安、再往西行，遂到達晉冀魯豫軍區司令部，住其牛頭村的招待所。旅行途中，每到大小村莊，都碰到很悲慘的土地改革流血鬥爭，地主被凌遲慘殺，家屬被流

放而沿途倒塌病餒，加上附近已有國民黨侵入或被佔領，所以心中很感五味雜陳，一個多月下來，根本無心來欣賞各地不同的景色。

　　同年四月，軍區組織部一個文化水準低，但是嚴正老實的資深幹部，來通知我上級要我組織一個「台灣隊」。不久，軍區政委鄧小平（四川人）及其政治敵工部張科長（忠實黨員，廣東人），把從劉鄧大隊七縱隊調下來的台灣兵二百多人交給我，黨中央並決定，一年之中將調下台灣兵五千人來受訓。因我林鐸不是黨員，所以是沒有隊長頭銜的隊長。

　　這些台灣兵，以不到二十歲的年輕人佔多數，到中國大陸後，人地生疏，言語不通，生活不習慣，裡頭都流傳著：「吃小米拉黃屎，快回台灣（吃白米）才會拉白屎。」對於歸鄉心情很著急。我聽到很揪心，為了安慰台灣同鄉的憂悶，常帶他們到山溝小溪去撈魚（華北平地池子的魚都不能吃，因帶有很濃的鹽份，只有鱉，但華北人叫著王八，也不吃），大家在心理上才稍有一點安歇。

　　同年七月，上級調來蔡公狄（廣東梅縣客家人，黨員，兩廣縱隊出身），我林鐸被正式任命為政治教員。到七月底，「台灣隊」從晉冀魯豫軍區司令部招待所出發，行軍三天二夜後，到河北省南宮縣（前九世紀是商紂王妾妃妲己之守城）的棗兒莊，在此正式成立「晉冀魯豫軍區台灣隊」，此時台灣隊的編制是：

　　隊長：蔡公狄

指導員：林施均（海南島人，黨員，延安抗日大學畢業，海
　　　　　南島與台灣在語言上稍微會通）

政治教員：林鐸（史明，台灣隊時上級屢次要我入黨，但我
　　　　　都推說學習還不夠，始終沒入黨）

政治教員：辛喬（東北吉林人，黨員，懂日本話，爲了偷聽
　　　　　台灣兵的談論，派來當教員，據聞他在瀋陽時是
　　　　　國民黨員，後赴延安進入抗日大學，最後在北京
　　　　　自殺）

　　到一九四八年六月，中共「人民解放軍」已從東北地區
與華北地區全面掃蕩國民黨軍，只剩下北京天津、太原及青
島等地區，以及一些小地方，黨中央即把晉察冀軍區與晉冀
魯豫軍區，統一爲「華北軍區」，「中央局」的第一書記是
劉少奇，第二書記薄一波，第三書記聶榮臻；軍區司令員則
是聶榮臻，政委薄一波，第一副司令徐向前，第二副司令滕
代遠，第三副司令蕭克。

　　早在同年四月，毛澤東、朱德、劉少奇、周恩來、任弼
時等黨中央領導幹部，已從延安轉移於華北軍區，毛澤東則
住在石家莊西北角的西柏坡南村。當時，在東北地區及華北
地區的國民黨軍已被掃蕩，只有留下北京天津、太原、青島
三處城市還在國民黨手裡。中共在第一次內戰時（1927-36）
在井崗山設立「紅軍大學」，抗戰時（1937-45）在延安繼爲
「抗日大學」，此時即把兩大學名稱合併爲「華北軍政大
學」，華北軍區總參謀長葉劍英兼任校長、校政委，蕭克任

副校長兼副政委,滕代遠任副校長兼副政委。

　　於是,「台灣隊」隨即從棗兒莊轉移於石家莊,以石家莊舊日軍西兵營為隊部,成為「華北軍政大學幹部總隊」第一大隊,直屬本校領導。台灣隊隊長蔡公狄,副隊長廖先景(新竹縣楊梅人,黨員,在前線立功,被稱為特等英雄,善阿諛奉承),**政治委員楊誠**(出身印尼的台灣人,黨員,廈門集美中學畢業,抗日大學畢業,在中央青年訓練班工作,據聞文革時被紅衛兵整死),**政委林施均,副隊長兼副政委張省吾**(棗兒莊村長兼書記,典型的黨官僚,土皇帝,據聞一九五七年時,在幕後指揮鬥爭謝雪紅),**政治幹事辛喬,政治幹事林鐸。後來從聯合大學調來教育幹事劉世英**(台灣岡山人,黨員),**教育幹事林漢章**(台灣宜蘭人,黨員),**教育幹事張文華**(台灣台南人,黨員),結果,在部隊幹部只有我林鐸一個人非黨員身份。

　　就這樣,台灣隊及其中每個台灣囝仔的生活,籠罩在罔顧人性的個人獨裁及陰險惡劣的土皇帝、獨裁的黨官僚主義中,被全面宰制。

　　不過,話說回來,台灣囝仔也真沒出息,一旦受到中共黨壓制,就爭先恐後去做黨員,互相分派系,搞內鬥的結果,自己打死一個嘉義人。

人民裁判・人間煉獄

　　一九三〇年代以來,中共就決定了所謂「農村政策」,一個鄉村定有共產黨「支部」,支部書記兼村長是村中唯一

的獨裁者，手中有黨民兵（武裝），他的土地都叫村民「代耕」，自己不幹活，作風蠻橫，村政府都控制在黨書記手裡，所以被蔑稱爲「土皇帝」。

我們撤退張家口的途中，到處看到沿路的佛像頭部都被砍掉，於是我問共黨幹部爲何會這樣，他們回答：「老百姓思想進步了，認爲宗教是鴉片，所以自動自發的把其頭砍掉。」到鄉村時，共黨都把工作人員分散住在老百姓家裡。我與住家的老百姓關係都很融洽，常常幫老百姓挑水做勞動，他們都把我看成是日本人。我所碰到的都是最貧苦最低層的中國老百姓，他們都毫無例外的純正樸實，都是很好的中國人。

有一天半夜，我起來到院子去撒尿，發現老百姓一家人手拿著香跪在地上拜天公，我嚇了一跳，他們也嚇了一跳。我問說：「你們連廟裡的佛像都給砍了頭，現在還在拜啥？」他們回答說：「那都是被共產黨逼的。」當時我聽到這句話，受到很大的衝擊。當天晚上翻來覆去睡不著覺，我自問：「馬克思那裡有這一套嗎？馬克思不是講要恢復人性嗎？怎麼會變成這樣？我到底在這裡要做的是什麼？我，一個台灣人，做的應該是怎樣的革命事業？」接連好幾天，我好像失魂落魄一樣，原來一天可走五、六十里路，這一下卻連一半路程也走不到。在途中想「不能再這樣下去了」，我自言自語的，對中共做法的疑問更加深一層。

中國社會在二千年來的封建帝王制，沒有革改過社會「體制」（二千年沒有革命，只有易姓）及清末以來的殖民地

性質的土地制度之下，農民大眾過著像在泥沼裡打滾的窮困生活。我在華北的多天，注意到對門的小夫妻，只要丈夫出門，太太一定留在家裡，太太出門，丈夫就留在家裡，後來問別人，才知道他們家窮得只能共用一條厚棉褲。大多數人每天喝小米粥、啃窩窩頭，很少有麵吃，佐配的頂好就是白菜豆腐，還不常有。

一九四六年中共公佈「土地改革」政策，開始土地改革鬥爭。其終極目標，不僅是給無地貧農分配土地，更加是要以毫無人性的鬥爭方法，快速消滅地主、重農、國民黨等人的肉體及階級。各村遂行所謂「土地改革」時，一定由黨中央局派來管督團，指示典型的流血鬥爭方法。我們親眼目睹的是把地主、重農白天叫到田裡幹活，晚上就開始鬥爭，無論男女，都吊起來以棍子打，叫他們坦白剝削佃農貧農的具體例子，並說出所有金條、龍銀藏在那裡，打得皮破血流也繼續亂打，這樣一次、二次、三次……，然後才召開所謂「人民裁判」。

人民裁判事先準備架子，把鬥爭對象顛倒吊上，架子右邊有靈桌，上面置佃農父母的神主牌，左邊桌上擺菜刀、剪刀、牛刀、羊刀、棍子等。然後敲鑼打鼓，動員村民男女老少全部出來開會，若不出來每一人要罰兩斤麻油，對生活極貧困的村民來說，一只雞蛋都很寶貴，哪能拿得出兩斤麻油，所以大家都零零落落、慢吞吞的出來，到廣場報名參加人民裁判。

我看到一次人民裁判，吊在架子的地主已被鬥了好幾

天，人都已經被打得黃酸，且是個纏腳的六、七十歲的婦人。主持裁判的「議長」就是黨支部書記兼村長，他一開始就叫出佃農向他們大聲的說：「你們的父親受了她的父親如何如何的凌遲，你自己又遭她壓榨一輩子，現在人民當家做主，是你訴苦和報仇的時候了……」，另一方面，安插在二百多個村民裡頭的黨員民兵就大聲嚷嚷，造成群眾壓力，在這火旺氣狂的氣氛下，佃農又驚又怕，跪在地上向父母靈桌邊哭邊拜。議長再接著大聲述說地主如何地苛酷剝削小農，最後說：「要如何處罰這反動的罪大惡極的地主？」各民兵就舉起槍桿子來喊：「槍斃！槍斃！」但又有聲音喊出：「這樣不夠！不夠！」遂有民兵接著喊：「要萬刀殺殺報仇致死才可以！」最後，議長說：「反對的舉手！」在這種情況下，誰敢舉反對的手呢？這樣就算是「老百姓的決定」。議長再向大家說：「每人用每樣殺一下，可以不可以？」民兵們同聲說：「可以，可以，決定，決定！」

但是什麼人要第一個下手，就成大問題了。因為村裡的人多半有親戚關係，大家都在閃避，所以就用抽籤的，結果一個男人抽到頭籤，得第一個下手選擇桌上的兇器殺人。可是他下不了手，只跪在廣場中央垂頭喪氣，此時，議長就經過婦女會，發動他的牽手出來罵他，她被逼得耍不過去，即罵他是沒勇氣、反革命，「你想要反共產黨，反人民裁判嗎？那我要跟你離婚了，你死好了。」就這樣，他的牽手哭哭啼啼，邊罵邊用拳頭打丈夫的腦袋，用腳踢他的背等等，要他去殺人民罪人的地主。同時，在旁的民兵們開始大聲起

鬨，整個廣場在民兵所喊的「殺殺殺」的肅殺之氣中，人心躁動不安。

　　這個抽到頭籤的人，遭到身邊氣氛的深深逼迫，終於忍不住突然站起來，把旁邊桌上的一根棒子搶在手中，一下子走近女地主身邊，把棒子又急又慌的向頭顱橫打一下，只聽到女地主哎的一聲，她的頭顱被打破了，紅色鮮血和白色腦漿都流出來，好似活地獄。接著，第二個、第三個……打人殺人就容易多了，有的用羊刀刺殺，有的用剪刀剪殺，有的用球棒打，有的割下她的耳朵、鼻子等等……。村民大多都用手掩目，不敢直視這活地獄的場景。我再次受到嚴重衝擊，原來自稱是社會主義革命部隊的共產黨，竟是面目猙獰的劊子手。

　　我那天飯也吃不下，睡也睡不著。房東一家四口，也靜悄悄的都沒吃飯。我整天躺在炕上，自問自答：「馬克思那裡有這玩意兒？馬克思不是講要消滅階級、恢復人性嗎？怎麼會搖身一變為這種慘世界？我到底在這裡要做的是什麼？我，不能這樣下去了，做的應該是和這個不同的解放革命！」一方面講，另方面卻想起台灣，思鄉之情油然而生。

　　所謂「毛澤東思想」是什麼？有一天在旅行途中，我忽然想毛澤東的詞〈沁園春‧雪〉：

　　　　北國風光，千里冰封，萬里雪飄，
　　　　望長城內外，惟余莽莽，大河山下，頓失滔滔，
　　　　山舞銀蛇，原馳蠟象，欲與天公試比高，

須晴日，看，紅裝素裹，分外妖嬈。

江山如此多嬌，引無數英雄競折腰，
惜，秦皇漢武，略輸文采，唐宗宋祖，稍遜風騷，
一代天驕，成吉思汗，只識彎弓射大鵰，
俱往矣，數，風流人物，還看今朝。

　　這篇文章是毛澤東一九三五年冬（四十三歲）帶領紅軍跋涉千水萬山，歷盡艱辛始達冰天雪地的延安時所作的詞。從這篇詞可以看出，他富於傷感事物，是一個文藻佳茂的浪漫吟詠詩人。但是這首詞更是暴露他所憧憬的，也不過是秦漢唐宋等昔古的皇帝罷了，其意識裡拂拭不去的，淨是封建時代的帝王思想。倘若是人民導師的毛澤東，道道地地站在勞苦大眾這一邊的話，心中懸念的，倒應該是老百姓口中膾炙的「孟姜女哭倒萬里長城」。我曾遊過山海關，去過「孟姜女廟」，其大門對聯：「白雲長，長長長，長長，長消。海水朝，朝朝朝，朝朝，朝退。」廣闊天空，靜靜流傳，悠悠意長。
　　總歸一句話，毛澤東的思想無非是中國帝王思想與斯大林獨裁主義的結合物。毛澤東從上而下的個人專制獨裁，更勝過中國歷代的皇帝，自恃為神聖而不可侵犯，其「無謬性」（不會發生錯誤）還遠超過歷代中國皇帝，這與要打破階級壓迫的社會主義理論完全相悖。

中國共產黨一黨獨裁

（一）馬克思主義

「共產黨宣言」

馬克思、恩格斯爲了恢復「人性」（認爲人性在資本主義下將會喪失），在「共產黨宣言」（1848），以科學方法創立「馬克思主義」（注重社會體制改革，說明資本主義將會崩潰，共產主義必會成立的社會法則），並以勞動者階級革命要實現共產主義。

「第一國際」：1864-76，西歐左翼各革命團體，統一爲國際勞動者協會，而做勞動者階級解放運動。

「第二國際」：1889-1914，團結萬國勞動者，期以勞動者階級政黨爭取各國政權。

第一次世界大戰時（1914-18），各國勞動者選擇保衛「祖國」，不走「階級路線」，第二國際分裂爲：

（1）「社會民主主義」路線：在解放勞動者階級的社會主義方法上，排除無產階級獨裁形態，斷然由議會主義實現社會主義「各盡所能，各取所得」。

（2）「列寧共產主義」路線：1917-1924，以武裝革命，達成共產主義，「各盡所能，各取所需」。

「第三國際」：列寧主張以武裝解決民族問題與農業問題，來打倒資本主義達成共產主義。

「斯大林暴力個人獨裁主義」：1928-1953，1924年列寧死後，斯大林繼承列寧的暴力革命，將其無限上綱發展爲個人獨裁的一黨專政及共產帝國主義，後來根據記載暗殺4、5千萬蘇聯國民。

「毛澤東主義」：1945年毛澤東取得中國共產黨主席地位後，把中國封建的「帝王思想」與現代暴力（法西斯）的「斯大林主義」結合在一起，以一黨個人獨裁制施行於中國，1945-1976年計殺害4千餘萬中國人。

（二）中國共產黨（簡稱「中共」）

「黨員」：2007年總數7,336萬人，黨員必須絕對服從黨領導。

「黨支部」：全國有320萬黨支部，黨員3人以上成立一黨支部，一村一黨支部，一居民委員會（一條街）一黨支部，官私各機關、各學校、各媒體、各企業……都要有一黨支部，支部書記由黨委內定任免。

「黨委」：黨委員會，黨支部的上級組織，承黨中央命令，領導所屬黨支部，委員由黨中央政治局內定任免。

「全國黨代表大會」：形式上是黨員選的「黨最高權力機構」，實際上是兩千餘人各地代表，人選均由黨中央政治局內定任免的虛構組織，五年召開一次會議。

「黨中央委員會」：形式上是全國黨代表大會選出並構成黨最高領導組織，實際上是2百餘名中央委員人選由黨中

央政治局內定任免。

「黨中央政治局」：中央委員會閉會中，代行其職權，實際上20餘人黨中央政治局委員由黨中央總書記內定任免。

「政治局常務委員」：形式上由黨中央政治局選出常務委員，實際上9人常務委員由黨中央總書記內定任免。

「黨中央總書記（主席）」：形式上由政治局常務委員互選，實際上是由前任總書記指定，如鄧小平任命江澤民，江澤民任命胡錦濤。

中共以上的組織系統，黨中央總書記及政治局常務委員必然成為最高領導獨裁者，黨、政及軍隊、警察等大權在握，成為一黨的獨裁者。

（三）中華人民共和國（簡稱「共和國」）

中共一黨獨裁專政

共和國只有中共一黨，其他所謂「政治協商會議」的許多政黨，都出自中共造成的花瓶黨，結果，政治權力均由中共一黨獨裁專政。

「全國人民代表大會」：形式上是人民選出代表的大會，實際上人民代表的絕大多數（90%）是黨政治局派出的中共黨員。

行政權：共和國政府主席是黨中央總書記兼任，總理、部長及中央、地方各高級職員必須以中共黨員充任，中央、地方各單位定要有「黨委」，各機關人事權、財政權都在各

黨委手裡，即政府官僚組織系統完全與一黨獨裁的共黨組織系統一體化，中共完全控制行政權。

共和國司法權：與行政權同樣在中共手中，由中央到地方的各檢察機關、公安警察以及裁判所等完全是黨員並由黨組織支配。

人民解放軍：屬黨中央軍事委員會領導，軍事委員會主席由黨中央總書記擔當，即軍總司令是黨中央總書記，軍人員必是黨員，結果，軍是黨軍而不是國軍。蔣介石中華民國的獨裁恐怖，但是毛澤東中華人民共和國一黨獨大更勝數倍厲害。

如此，中國共產黨透過黨組織完全掌握共和國政府的行政權、司法權以及軍隊、警察等政治權力，實行完全一黨獨裁的政治支配。

1953年斯大林死亡，1976年毛澤東死亡，1990年蘇聯政府與蘇聯共產黨垮台，之後，所謂原本的馬克思主義受到致命性打擊，然而世界上的共產國家，仍然各在斯大林主義一黨獨裁政治體制之下。原始馬克思主義與斯大林、毛澤東的一黨獨裁共產主義不同。

另一方面，從第一次世界大戰後，發展起來的社會民主主義革命運動，在德國及北歐四國，或英國系各國家，成為長期當政的自由民主國家系統。社會主義與共產主義不同。

美蘇冷戰時期，東西的對立，在理論上體制上，是資本主義與斯大林共產主義的對立，更是自由世界與非自由世界的對立，民主主義與獨裁主義（法西斯）的對立。

1. Crossing the Red Tide

Translated by Ching-Chih Chen (陳清池)

In 1942, I decided that after graduating from Waseda University I would go to the Chinese Mainland in September to participate in the anti-imperialist Resist-Japan war. Before I made that decision, in April of that year I arrived in Shanghai and then traveled to take a look at the area librated by the New Fourth Army. I found out later that it was the "Huainan Huanghuatang Base" that I visited. In June, I returned to Taiwan for a farewell visit to my aged grand-mother, but of course I did not let her know that I had planned to take part in the Resist-Japan War in China.

At the time, I was a young man very well taken cared by my family. I lived freely, comfortably and without responsibility for others whatsoever. In retrospect, it is likely that I was more naïve than my peers of the time for I had not come into contact with real world and thus had no knowledge how evil some people can be. Having graduated from college, my head was full of Marxist ideas. I thought that by joining the Chinese Communist Party's Resist-Japan troops I would be able to implement the liberation philosophy of Marxism that I had learned from books.

The Call of Marxism

In my sophomore and junior years at Weseda University, I studied diligently Marxist theory. Marx advocated class liberation as the basis of his theory. However, during the time of the First International, Marxists, particularly Marx and Engles, understood well the political significance of the struggle for national independence of the oppressed nations. At the time, the First International's support for national struggle was primarily for the national liberation revolution of Europe's dependant nations such as Poland, Ireland and Italy. Marx also had actively studied the national revolution of various nations in the East. He had some understanding of China's Incident of the Taiping Heavenly Kingdom (1851-64). He wrote, "The Chinese revolution threw the flame into the ammunitions depot of industrial organizations. It thus led to the explosion of long simmering crises and further contributed the outbreak of closely related European political revolutions." In addition, Marx wrote in his "Das Capital" stressing the importance of liberating various colonies in Asia. In 1883, Engels also predicted anti-colonial revolutions in India, Persia, Egypt and other colonies.

In 1920, the second conference of the Third International met in Moscow. At the time, Lenin had already become the great teacher and director of the global labor movement. Participating in the conference were representatives from 35 countries and 42 branches throughout the world. The conference adopted a series of political, organizational and operational measures. However, the foremost political issue of the conference was Lenin's proposed bill titled "Guidelines for National and Colonial Issues". In his speech at the conference, Lenin said "together with the proletarian revolution of the mother country, the dissolution of the colonial empires will break up the Capitalist system of Europe." "There are two kinds of nations, the oppressors and the oppressed. About 70% of the people on planet Earth are the oppressed … A major source of the energy of European Capitalist countries is to be found in the colonies and dependant states. Capitalist powers cannot exist even for an instance if they do not widely rob and exploit their colonies."

Initially, Lenin's idea was to launch from Europe. He therefore actively supported revolution of the laborers in Hungary, Germany and other countries. However, the Hungarian revolution of 1919 failed. And, the Spartacus League (German Communist Party), which was established by Polish Rosa Luxemburg in Germany, was defeated. Luxemburg and other revolutionaries lost their lives. Lenin consequently realized that it was extremely difficult for European revolutions to succeed in Europe where capitalism was strong. It was necessary to place the focus of world proletarian revolution in colonies where capitalist force was weak and to support revolutionary movement in the colonies. Consequently, the Third International began to emphasize the task of supporting the "colonial liberation and national independence" of colonies and dependant countries in Asia and Africa. For examples, there were established Korean Communist Party in 1920, Chinese Communist Party in 1921, and Japanese Communist Party in 1922. In addition, it helped to bring about the cooperation between the Nationalists and Communists in China in 1924. Under such situation, Xie Xuehong and Lin Muxun arrived in Moscow in 1926 to receive Communist training. After returning to Shanghai, Xie and Lin established Taiwanese National Branch of the Japanese Communist Party, i.e. the Taiwanese Communist Party, in 1928. The strategy of the Third International was thus through supporting the independence of colonies to bring about the collapse of Capitalist empires and the success of the world's proletarian revolution.

My Japanese classmates in the political science department at Waseda University were duty-bound to enter military service. After graduation, they were very determined to enlist as members of the Kamikaze Special Attack Unit in order to fight to death in the service of their country and emperor. Their determination and acts deserved respect. In contrast, while I did not have to serve in the military, I felt a sense of emptiness. At the time, anti-colonialist and colonial liberation movement was the most progressive and popular thing to do. After much deliberation, I decided to go to China to participate in the Resist-Japan of "Anti-imperialist Struggle". This way I would be striving for the liberation of Taiwan and proletarian classes. It was out of a sudden and not so-well-thought process that made my decision to go to the liberated area controlled by the Chinese Communist Party.

Therefore, it was not out of Han Chinese consciousness that I decided to go to China. It was because of Marxist view that I opposed Japanese imperialism. I had never considered joining Chiang Kaishek's Nationalist Party (or Kuomintang and hereafter KMT in short) army. In my view, Chiang was a Chinese warlord and the KMT was a feudal league of landlords and evil gentry. They retreated to China's great interior and had no intention of fighting the Japanese at all.

Nothing to Do with Chinese Nation

When I was a junior at Waseda University, I accidentally joined a secret Marxist Book Club through the introduction of a Japanese classmate Ooshiba Shigeo. After the Second World War, this classmate of mine became a member of House of Representatives representing Socialist Party. This book club had 7 Japanese students who did not know each other's names or which school each attended. We studied

Marxism, Marxist strategy and tactics, etc. At the Club, I met a Chinese student Shen (not his real name). Later, I learned that he was sent by the Chinese Communist Party (hereafter CCP in short) to Japan as an underground agent. I ultimately decided to ask him to guide me to visit the CCP-controlled liberated area in North China.

I truly believed in Karl Marx's view on national issues, namely "When the problem of social classes is resolved, the problem of nations will be solved." At the time, like the average Taiwanese, I knew that our ancestors came from the Chinese Mainland. Taiwanese and Chinese shared the same culture and same race. However, Taiwanese did not have "Chinese nation" consciousness and sensitivity. There were really no contacts between Taiwan and China in the past 400 years. There were no social relations. Taiwan existed in near isolation. During the Qing Dynasty period, there were only Qing bureaucrats and big merchants could travel between in Taiwan and the Chinese mainland. During the period of Japanese colonial rule, the average Taiwanese rarely met Chinese and had never visited China. The Taiwanese who visited Chinese places such as Amoy accounted for a very small number in the total population. The majority of such people were either smugglers or students. In China's vast territory, the typical Chinese had no concept of Taiwan. For instance, when I was in North China in 1948, I met Chinese farmers who asked me where I was from. To my answer "Taiwan", they said, "That is a place north of Korea, right? (They meant Japan.)"

My going to China had nothing to do with the national issue between Taiwan and China. Based on my philosophy of life, I had two choices: work so as to make a living and enjoy pleasure or struggle for society, nation (Taiwanese), social classes, etc. I ultimately chose the second option.

Full of ambitions and passions, I wanted to leave Japan for China to participate in the Resist-Japan War. However, throughout my twenty-plus-years of wonderful experiences living in the Japanese style environment, I had truly enjoyed beautiful sceneries, appreciated elegant Japanese culture, and was nostalgic about memorable experiences of associating with Japanese classmates, university professors and others in the society. (Japanese imperialist rule in Taiwan was indeed brutal and harsh. Japanese, however, had little sense of colonial superiority over Taiwanese. They were friendly when dealing with Taiwanese individually.) Memories of the past flashed quickly back and forth in my mind. Grandmother's face jumped up in front of my eyes and greatly saddened me. But, I had managed to put life and death issue aside.

It was now time to get on the road.

My Years in Suzhou and My First Salary

I did not attend the September, 1942 commencement ceremony at Waseda. Instead, I hurriedly took the train from Tokyo to Nagasaki to catch the 10,000-ton ship, Nagasaki Maru, bound for China. On the train and aboard the ship, I looked out of the window at the passing scenery. The sad feeling of separation from relatives and friends arose once more.

The morning of my second day on the ship, a Japanese passenger said, "We are almost there." Looking down the side of the ship, the deep blue sea water was now replaced by torrents of river water. The ship had entered the Yangtse River. After another half a day, the ship sailed into Huangpu River. Finally, there was the Garden Bridge over the Suzhou River and the Broadway Mansion on the river bank of Suzhou River. Further in, Pudong was on the right and Waitan on the left. Along the way was row after row of high-rise buildings owned by Jews from Britain. The ship anchored at Waitan.

The man who came on board the ship to meet me was Zhu Bin (not his real name) of Shanghai. He immediately led me to Suzhou to move into a room for one person. The next day, he took me to a police station to apply for household registration card. In this way I easily became a "Chinese". Thereafter, I used a series of names such as Shi Ming, Lin Ming and Lin Fan. Due to the fact that after arriving in Suzhou I didn't visit the Japanese consulate, I automatically relinquished my Japanese household status and officially abandoned Japanese citizenship.

After more than ten days in Suzhou, Zhu Bin took me to Zhengjiang, wherefrom we crossed the river to arrive at Yangzhou. The original plan was for me to go north by following the route of the Seventh Army to reach the liberated area in North China. North of the Yangtze River was then the liberated area of the New Fourth Army with Chen Yi as its commanding general. After four or five days of walking I was surprised to find myself back in Suzhou. Later I was told that the Chinese Communists had realized that I looked like a Japanese and wanted me to work undercover gathering Japanese military and political intelligence in Suzhou that was the headquarters of a major Japanese military unit with 130,000 Japanese troops and had many major offices.

The political situations of the time were complicated. Wang Jingwai was originally Sun Yatsen's revolutionary right-hand man. He served as the head of the executive branch of the original Nanjing government. In 1938, he escaped to Hanoi from Kunming that was then under the jurisdiction of Chiang Kaishek's Chungqing government. In Hanoi Wang dispatched a telegraph announcing his plan to cooperate with the Japanese imperialists. In March 1939 he set up a puppet regime the "Nationalist government of the Republic of China" in the Japanese occupied Nanjing. The government advocated "Sino-Japanese friendship and anti-Communist alliance" and negotiated peace with Japan. As for Suzhou, it was the provincial capital of Jiangsu Province set up by former Chiang Kaishek followers such as Ding Motun and Li Shiqun who had surrendered to the Japanese and were performing the task of "Cleansing the Countryside." The previous provincial governor was Chen Qun, of Fuzhou, Fujian while a later successor was Ren Yuandao, of Yixing, Jiangsu.

I was in Suzhou from 1942 to 1945. At the time, the head of the Provincial Bureau of Education was Yuan Su who was actually an underground Chinese Communist cadre. He recommended me to work at a provincial economic unit. In reality, I was only required to report to the office once a week, but was paid without having to work. This was the first time I was paid a salary. Even though I had nominally started holding a government job, I could not speak either Mandarin or Suzhou dialect. At first, to communicate with others, I either used hand gesture or wrote Chinese characters. I began to learn Chinese bo-po-mo pronunciation system as the tool to speak Mandarin. As Taiwanese and Mandarin share the same writing script, the Mandarin was rather easy to learn. Besides, I did work hard to learn. For example, every day while walking in town, I would recite in Mandarin street names along the way. As for the Suzhou dialect, to this day I cannot speak it. However, I did frequent downtown area to have delicacies such as eight-ingredient rice and wrapped steamed-rice.

There were not many Taiwanese residing in Central China then. Among these Taiwanese, the better-known ones were: Li Yingzhang who led the sugar cane farmers anti-Japanese incident in Erlin and changed his name to Lin Waiguang to serve as the Chinese Communist liaison man in Shanghai; Li Yubang of Heshangchou, Taipei who led several tens of Taiwanese volunteer soldiers and in Jinhua, Zhejiang he served as Chiang Kaishek's KMT Army broker in dealing with the Japanese troops; Lan Guocheng sereved as chief of staff of Wang Jingwai government army in Nanjing; Wang Porung and Lin Kunzhang founded Zhung Ya Bank in Shanghai; and other anti-Japanese men such as Yang Zhaojia and Yangbai Chengzhi in Shanghai's French concession.

In the summer of 1943, I went to Xiamen to visit relatives. After staying there for half a month, Communist organization in Xiamen asked me to take along a Chinese woman named "A-yun" and a man named Chen Wu back to Shanghai. In Shanghai, I and A-yun acted as a couple living near Beisi Pagoda in Suzhou. Concerned that A-yun's pregnancy might hinder our revolutionary work later, I hastily decided to have a vasectomy at a Japanese medical clinic on North Sicuan Road in Shanghai. The surgery thus ended for good any hope of my having biological children.

With the intention of avoiding military service, my younger brother Lin Chaoyang came to Shanghai.

Later, however, he enlisted with Japanese Army headquarters in Nanjing and frequently came to visit me in Suzhou. Wu Ketai also came to stay over-night in my Suzhou house quite often. (Wu later became a director of standing committee of Taiwan Democratic Self-rule Alliance in the Chinese Communist controlled region. He was from Yilan and his original name was Jan Shiping. He was my brother Chaoyang's classmate at Taipei Second High School. Then he volunteered to join the Japanese army and was sent to Shanghai to serve as an interpreter for the army headquarters. Allegedly he often witnessed the Japanese killing of KMT's undercover agents.)

Decadent Life while Gathering Intelligence

It was said that in 1938 the CCP Center established the "Southeast Bureau" and had Xiang Ying as the Bureau secretary. (Xiang came from Wuhan City, Hubei, was the deputy commander of the New Fourth Army and later died in the Huannan (southern Anhui) Incident.) The Bureau was in charge of underground work in the KMT-controlled Jiangsu, Zhejiang, Anhui and Jiangxi. In 1941 after the Huannan Incident, the Southeast Bureau became East Bureau under the leadership of Zhou Enlai and Dung Piwu. At the time the underground work of the Communist army in Shanghai was fully under the charge of Pan Hannian,

Fang Fang and Li Kenong.

Pan Hannian was from Yixing, Jiangsu. He was the editor-in-chief of "Hongsui (Great Flood)" published by the Creative Society founded by Guo Moruo and Cheng Fanwu. Later he was the first secretary of Cultural Work Committee directly affiliated with the CCP Central, and head of Liaison Department of the Central China Bureau. During and after the Resist-Japan War, he was in Shanghai and Hong Kong secretly doing underground work and coming into contacts with members of the anti-Chiang and anti-Communist "Third Party" for their joint effort in resisting Japan and saving China. During the later part of the Liberation War, he brought over 350 of so called "Enlightened Gentlemen" to safely reach the liberated area under the guise of "New Political Consultation Conference". He then served as the deputy mayor of Communist Shanghai. In 1955, however, having been suspected of treason, he was arrested for investigation. After his death, his reputation was restored in 1982.

While in Suzhou, I learned of various pieces of intelligence from Communist underground agents. The intelligence agency of Japanese occupation army Nodori Division was in Suzhou. Through the introduction of layers of Communist underground agents, I came to know Japanese spy chief Nagadashima Kanichi (made-up name Matsui). Getting friendly with him, I was able to collect intelligence. I had frequent contacts with Japanese spies in Suzhou,

Shanghai, Nanjing and other places. Simultaneously, with underground agents Lan Tien, Li Kan and others we rented a private house as the underground liaison place in the alley across from Shanghai's famous Dashijie (Great World). With Japanese military personnel, we drank, danced, and played with prostitutes. In a nutshell, we lived decadent life daily.

In Shanghai, Japanese Navy had a "Military Attaché" Colonel Ogasawara who was a friend of my father. In Jiangyin, there was Marine Corps Captain Udo who graduated from Waseda University after a few years after I did. These Japanese officers were all sources of my intelligence gathering. In addition, I was able to learn from Chen Baocuan about intelligence gathered from Japan's intelligence units. I was consequently quite productive in collecting Japanese military intelligence.

Chen Baocun was someone I made friend of during this time. Chen was from Bangga, Taiwan. After his graduation from Manzhouguo's Academy of Law and Politics, he was dispatched to Suzhou to work under Matsui's intelligence unit. The Academy specialized in training bureaucrats for the puppet Manzhouguo government. Many Taiwanese studied there. Chen assumed low posture with others, but he was hypocritical. What he claimed to be his credentials and experiences were largely untrue. His wife, however, understood well the ways of the world. After Japan's defeat, Chen flattered members of the Dai Li military faction who were sent from Chungqing to take over Japanese intelligence organizations in Taiwan. He was immediately employed by Dai Li faction and dispatched back to Taiwan to do spy work. He also worked at Taiwan University in the area of student disciplining. With his background in intelligence, he would proceed to serve as National Assemblyman, and later chairman of the board of different banks and a major insurance company. He was the godfather of Chiang Chingkuo's illegitimate son Channg Hsiaochih. One can thus see that his previous involvement in the spy network benefitted in his rise to high and profitable positions.

After my return to Taiwan in 1949, Chen Baocun introduced me to Gao Liwen (Suwen) a classmate of Chiang Chingkuo during their stay in the Soviet Union. Gao managed newspapers for Chiang Chingkuo in Kannan (Southern Jiangsi). When Chiang was combating criminals in Shanghai, Gao arrested (on behalf of Chiang) Kung Xiangxi's son who was later released by Chiang Chingkuo himself. In Taiwan Gao was a senior adviser at the Central Trust. However, he distasted the lawlessness of the four Big Families of Chiang, Kung, Song and Chen. He opposed the fascist secret police politics of the two Chiangs. For that, secret police put surveillance on him. He later migrated to the US.

During the Spring and Autumn Period, Suzhou was part of the state of Wu. Then in the Sui and Tang era, the construction of the Grand Canal contributed to the development of commerce and handicraft industry in Suzhou. Nationally-known scenic and historical spots such as Beisi Pagoda, Shizi Forest, Hanshan Temple, and Hu Hill emerged so much that poets throughout the ages wrote about the city and praise its beauty. With the Yangtse River to the east of the city, Lake Tai to the west, Suzhou, as described in Marco Polo's Travel Account, was "a solid and lovely major city. Its residents produced large amount of raw silk which was not only used to make silk clothes but also for shipping to markets elsewhere." Inscribed on a stela in Hanshan Temple of Suzhou is "Night Stay at Maple Bridge" by Zhang Ji:

> *The moon sets, a crow caws,*
> *   and frost all over the sky,*
> *Maple leaves and fishing boats float on the river,*
> *   but I am having a sleepless night.*
> *Hanshan Temple outside of Suzhou City,*
> *The chimes of mid-night bells reach the boat's*
> *   passengers.*

Shanghai was the cosmopolitan center of the so-called "World's Colony." It was divided into French concession, Japanese concession and joint leased territory of major powers. Extra-territoriality was so prevalent that Shanghai had become a world-class harbor full of westerners and was abound with western atmosphere. Foreign ships frequented the harbor. Heavy industry and commerce were well developed. Many Chinese in Shanghai served as compradors to the foreign merchants. They pursued the life style of luxury and vanity. They might look happy but were actually frivolous. At the time, entrance to parks in the French concession had posted signs saying "Dogs and Chinese are not allowed." In the suburb of Shanghai, there was KMT's Nation-saving Army led by the KMT military faction's spys Zhou Weilong, Ma Zhichao and Mao Shen.

Whenever I visited Shanghai, what I liked most was to go to Peking opera performances. I loved performances of such established performers as Chi Lintong, Zhang Junqiu and Lin Shushen. While watching the show, I would reminisce accompanying my mother to attend Peking opera performance at Taipei's New Theater located at Duadiudia/Tadaochen district. I was then already a theater fanatic. In the French Concession, there was the foreign-managed Lyceum Theatre that produced ballet performances such as Russian composer Igor Stravinsky's "The Firebird." Such musical performances pleased both my ears and eyes.

An incredible incident occurred when I was in Shanghai.

One day, I was walking on the popular Nanjing Road near where the French Concession met the International Jointly-leased Area. Absent-mindedly I stepped on the foot of a Chinese man. I apologized to the man, as I would have done in Taiwan and Japan. However, I was surprised that the man immediately jumped up to grab my tie and at the same time shouted loudly in Shanghai dialect that I did not understand. He must be cursing why I stepped on his foot. As he cursed bitterly, I could only say "Sumimasen (sorry)" in Japanese to apologize to him repeatedly. I was also greatly surprised by the fact that pedestrians nearby quickly surrounded us in layers to see what was going on. I made my apology again. This way it went on for nearly an hour. As I had never experienced such embarrassment before, suddenly an idea came to my mind that I could probably use money to solve the problem. I took a wallet out of my pocket. Right away the man took the money and left as if nothing had happened. The mass of spectators also dispersed quickly. It was so unfathomable to me that as soon as I returned to my residence in Shanghai, I told my roommate and friend what happened to me in details. What further amazed and surprised me was that my friend said that it was my fault. He said that it was wrong for me to apologize to the man. He suggested that I should have said to the man, "Fuck you! Why did you stretch your foot out so far that you made me step on it? Go away, go away…" I felt extremely uneasy listening to what my roommate said to me. Why?

In Shanghai, I wore Hong Kong shirt and Western suit and so did men of Shanghai. The city-scape is no

different from that of other big cities. However, what
happed to me made me realize for the first time that
the Chinese and Taiwanese were so different.

Maoism at Changjiakou

In November, 1945, the CCP underground
organization in Shanghai asked me to pick up opium
in Beijing. The Chinese Communists had been
planting opium poppies in North China, Mongolia
and Xinjiang. Opium was shipped to Shanghai,
Tianjin and then transferred to other places for sale.
The profit from opium was the major revenue to be
used for underground activities. As early as 1936,
for the purpose of invading China, Japan first used
Manzhoguo to attach Inner Mongolia. This military
move drove Warlord Fu Zeyi's military corps from
Sueiyuan, and compelled Mongolian King Goode
to jointly form with Li Shouxin, a Han Chinese, the
"Government of Mongolia and Xinjiang." Then in 1937
Japan engineered the Sino-Japanese Incident. After
Japan lost the war, Chinese Communists took over
the government and renamed as Jun-Cha-Ji Border
Region Government. At the same time, they took over
the cultivation, manufacturing and marketing of opium
by establishing an Opium Prohibition Bureau to control
the opium enterprise. When the Japanese army
occupied North China and established North China
Political Affairs Committee with Wang Keming as its

director, the Chinese Communists utilized Jin-pu and Jing-Han two major north-south railroads as well as the sea route from Tienjin to Shanghai and got Japanese troops to ship opium to distribute to areas controlled by the KMT and to Southeast Asia.

When Japan surrendered on August 15, 1945, in order to prevent American-supplied and American-armed KMT army from advancing north to occupy North China, the Chinese Communists destroyed overnight the two major north-south railroads to completely sever transportation between North and South. Since there was no railroad to transport opium, the CCP asked me to set up a station in the North. Much earlier when my father was the head of Bureau of Monopoly in Xiamen, I was absolutely opposed to my father's addiction to opium. Recalling the past, I must have been so overzealous for the "revolution" that as if under spells I subserviently obeyed the Communist order to help ship opium.

In September, 1945, Chiang Kaishek dispatched the leader of Guangxi Faction Commander Li Zhungzen to occupy Beijing. The person who ordered me to fetch opium was affiliated with Jun-Cha-Ji Military Region while the person who handed opium to me belonged to Jun-Ji-Lu-Yu Military Region. I arrived in Beijing to receive opium and then to immediately hand it over to the next person to take to Shanghai. However, for unknown reason I was unable to contact the person and had to wait in Beijing till February of the following year to make connection with two underground agents (Ju and Bo) from Jun-Ji-Lu-Yu Region.

Beijing had been the political and cultural center of China for nearly a thousand years. The city has Forbidden (Imperial) Palace, Summer Palace, Heavenly Altar and other well-known scenic and historical spots. In particular, the Forbidden Palace was built of red bricks and green tiles and has been widely seen as a rare heritage of the world. To me, however, what attracted me most is nothing but Peking opera. During the three or four months my stay in Beijing, I concentrated on enjoying brilliant opera performances. I really had a great time.

In June, 1936, Edgar Snow, the author of "Red Star over China" (first published in 1937), visited Mao Zedong in Yanan. In his interview of Mao, Mao agreed that Korea and Taiwan should become independent. In May, 1943, the Third International was dissolved. In April, 1945, the CCP convened its Seventh Conference of Party Representatives. With the support of Liu Shaoqi and others, Mao was elected chairman of the CCP. As a result, he had collected for himself power over the party, government and military and began his own dictatorship. (Liu Shaoqi was struggled to death by Mao during the Cultural Revolution.) At the time, the "Military Affairs Committee of the CCP" was the supreme agency of the Communist military. The Committee's Chairman was Mao, Deputy Chairmen were Zhu De, Zhou Enlai, Liu Shaoqi and Yeh Jianying.

Chu De was the Commander of the Eight Route Army (later renamed People's Liberation Army), Deputy Commander Peng Dehuai and Chief of Staff Yeh Jianying.

Inexperienced, simple and rather dumb, I took the big step out and severed my tie with the past. I began a new life in the cold climate of North China and partook in the dangerous underground activities. Thereafter I assumed the fake name of Lin Tuo.

In November, 1945, through the introduction of Jun-Ji-Lu-Yu underground agents, I flew an American amphibian plane from Shanghai Longhua Airport to Qingxao, and from there I transferred to an airplane of the Chinese Airlines to arrive in Beijing. In March, 1946, I rode KMT-controlled Pingsuai Railroad originating from Peking to Zhangjiakou, but got off at Kangzhuang. By way of the Zhuyongguan Gate which was then under neutral hands, I rode a horse carriage to arrive in Jun-Cha-Ji (Shanxi, Chahaer and Hobei provinces) Communist liberated military area. The military commander and political commissar was Nie Rongchen while deputy commander was Xia Ke. The head of Labor Department was Liu Ren (later served as deputy mayor of Beijing. The Red Guards struggled him to death during the Cultural Revolution.)

Accompanied by my Japanese girl friend Hilaka Kyoko, whom I met in Beijing where she was an employee at the Japanese Embassy, I arrived at Zhangjiakou where the Central Bureau of Jun-Cha-Ji military region was located. (The major officials of the Bureau were Nie Rongchen, Peng Chen and Liu Ren.) My first impression of Zhangjiakou was that everywhere one turned one saw wall posters with slogans such as "Long Live Chinese Communist Party", "Mao's Three Great Policies" (Base, Land Reform and Guerilla Warfare), "Bear arms to march to the battle front and carry plows to cultivate the fields", etc. We stayed in the guesthouse, but we were prohibited from moving around freely. There were little fellows everywhere watching us. It was shocking and truly unreasonable. Life there was so different and un-free.

In April, 1946, Hilaka and I were taken to register in tutorial class at the United University, whose president was Chen Fangwu. At the time many intellectuals teaching at Lu Xun's Academy of Arts in Yanan were sent to teach at United University. Among them were Ding Ling (a well-known poetess), Xiao Jun (a favorite student of Lu Xun who while alive was considered an imperialist pawn but after death he was regarded as a cultural patriot), Xiao San (a poet who studied in the Soviet Union and was a Communist cadre), and Ai Qing (a well-known poet). The teachers often invited me to talk with them for they knew and valued the fact that I was the only one who had voluntarily come from Taiwan while the three other Taiwanese were captured while serving in the Japanese troops.

The United University had a lot of young students from regions either under KMT or Japanese control.

Ten plus students were assigned to a class/group to share a dorm room. Every day, they had toufu and white cabbage soup to go with their millet rice. Due to my inability to adapt and acclimatize, I could not eat and hence my health deteriorated. In addition, I had hemorrhoids. One day as I was in a squat toilet without a door, some student saw I was bleeding heavily. Having learned about my health problem, teachers such as Ding Ling and Xiao Jun often came to visit me and even took me to the teachers' cafeteria to enjoy better food. These people had some humanitarian sentiment, but the Communist Party considered humanitarianism is a capitalist idea and is thus counter-revolutionary. That was the first problem I encountered in the liberated area. In Yanan of 1941, Mao Zedong through his "Talk on Literature and Arts" and "Rectification Movement" publicly criticized Ding Ling and Xiao Jun for their intellectual and petty bourgeoisie ideas. They were subsequently exiled to Northeast China.

During my time at the United University, as a class we read daily Mao's writings such as "New Democracy" and "On United Government", Lenin's "Country and Revolution", and the newspaper "Liberation Daily". In the day time, we meet to discuss while in the evening we had to engage in self-criticism or write autobiography. Sometimes the entire student body of over one thousand gathered to listen to lecture on "Historical Materialism". However, I found the lecturer's theoretical background to be far inferior to that of lecturers at Japanese universities. For example, it was unbelievable to hear that it was counter-revolutionary for the U.S. to possess nuclear bombs while it was revolutionary if the Soviet Union had the bombs. Another example, Marxism started from wanting to restore "humanity" that had been lost because of Capitalist thought and system. And, this was the liberation ideology. However, since our arrival in the liberated area, we had been watched closely. And, whenever we had the opportunity to leave the campus ground, we had to be accompanied by the class leader or the arms-bearing little guards. All of this mystified me. (This was the product of Mao Zedong's dictatorship and it clearly violated the socialist principle.)

My First Taste of Guerilla Fighting

During the Resist-Japan War, in the KMT-controlled area south of the Yangtse River, there were many young students who responded to Chiang Kaishek's call for "One Million Young Men, One Million Troops" by joining the KMT army to fight the war against Japan. However, all those who were fighting the Japanese troops were Communist guerilla forces in areas north of the Yangtse River. The KMT Army rarely fought the Japanese. After Japan's defeat, Chiang Kaishek immediately moved his government from Chongqing back to Nanjing. Soldiers, bureaucrats and others rushed to places formerly occupied by the Japanese so as to take over or plunder, for their individual use, vast structures and properties left behind by the Japanese. In the meantime, a large number of young students and soldiers had been abandoned or forced to de-enlist. Subsequently many of those who had no way to return home joined the Communist forces for they had been attracted by the Communist promise that in the Communist liberated area "when there are meals all get to eat, and when there are jobs to do all work together. It is one's freedom to choose whether to work or to study." Many left from Xi'an, Beijing, Tianjin or other places for the Communist liberated areas. I met many such people at the United University.

The peace talk between the Nationalists and Communists, with the "three men group" of U.S. General Marshall, Nationalist Zhang Qun and Communist Zhou Enlai, ended in failure. In July, 1946, the Civil War between the Nationalists and the Communists broke out. Stationing in the Northeast were 10 plus divisions of American-equipped Nationalist troops. Divided into two main groups, they planned to seize Zhangjiakou and to restore Pingsuei Railroad so as to sever Communist forces in North China from the Northeast. Under the protection of the Communist 129th Division led by Chen Zaidao and with the cooperation of local armed units, the Jun-Cha-Ji Central Bureau and other governments units withdrew from Zhangjiakou to march toward Fuping. As they marched along the way, these personnel of government units and the Communist troops that protected them had to fight against the KMT troops. During a three-month period, for the first time I participated in guerilla war. We then arrived in Lingqiu in northern Shansi Province.

While the march stopped temporarily in Lingqiu, I, after deliberation, requested my superiors to allow me to learn military affairs. The organization dispatched me to Yingxian to enter the Infantry School. The School was the highest military school in Jun-Cha-Ji Military Region and was specifically set up for the reeducation and training of middle-grade military cadre coming from the battle front. The military students all had many fighting experiences, but most of them had been recruited from rural villages and were nearly illiterate. While their cultural level was low, they were honest, sincere and simple. After having been admitted to the school, I studied with them guerilla warfare, Mao Zedong Thought, discipline, and skills in leading the soldiers, etc. I got along well with them. Sometimes, I got excited just listening to their talking proudly about their battle-field experiences.

After three months of training at the Infantry School, I was called back to do research work at the Resource Office of the Jun-Cha-Ji-Mon-Jiang Bank. I also did some transporting assignments with the donkey transport team. During the march, the troops and the United University corps traveled together on and off. We had frequent contacts with the university students from the KMT-controlled area. We also had opportunity of staying in the same village. We did accidentally bump into villagers working on land reform and having anti-KMT "People's Court".

In 1946 the CCP Central authority in Yanan promulgated "May 4th Instruction" and "Anti-KMT Spies". The villages were ordered to carry out land reform and eliminate KMT members. The land reform was an attempt to transform China from a feudalistic society to a communist society. However, the Communist Party not only took the land from the landlords but also destroyed their lives. Some of them were beaten to death, while others were killed by slicing to death. Even family members could not escape the misfortune. Such rectification movement exposed the ugly and evil nature of the Chinese Communist dictatorship. At the time, the Communist Party divided the masses into landlords, rich peasants, middle peasants and poor peasants four major classes. Landlords and rich peasants were the target of the struggle. The Party Central sent a team of supervisors to each village to promote and supervise the land reform. They used extremely brutal measurers to destroy the lives of landlords, rich peasants and KMT members. Relatives of the victims would be banished. They would be forced to wear badges identifying them as relatives of a named landlord and then driven out of their home town. No one in the neighboring villages would dare to take them in, but instead allowed them to die of starvation on the roadside. The Communist members regularly stressed that the defendant's crime implicated the entire clan. It was then that I fully understood the meaning of the term.

However, the students who arrived in the Chinese Communist liberated area from KMT-controlled territory were mostly from families of landlords, capitalists or middle and small merchants. During their time at the United University, they had come under pressure of continuous compulsory criticism and consequently were discouraged and dispirited. And then, after having seen the people's trials of landlords and KMT members that resulted in deaths and other bloody brutality, they became fearful and depressed. For those who could not endure the shocks, they attempted to run away. Chinese Communist organization and administration were tight and strict. Any one moving in and out was required to have a pass issued by their working units. Deserters without passes inevitably would be caught by the Communist branch militia of neighboring villages and sent back the morning of the following day to the village from which they had escaped from. The Communist cadres would beat badly the recaptured deserters. There were some who would still attempt to escape for the second time, third time and so on. Ultimately, some found it so intolerable that they jumped in an old well to commit suicide.

I saw with my own eyes such tragic events. There was this particular case: early one day morning we were washing faces and brushing teeth around the well. We lowered the water bucket to the well to fetch water, but instead we brought up the body of a young man whom I had talked with only a few days ago. One more body was brought up that day. And both bodies were bended. Seeing such sad situations, I lost hope in the Chinese Communists. I was so shocked that I could not even eat.

I pondered back and forth over the situation. Recalling the lectures at the United University, I realized that I had been participating in the exploitation of others. Suddenly I realized "Not being Chinese, I have a way out. If I were to die, I would prefer to die in Taiwan." Thus there emerged my decision to return to Taiwan.

Popular song had to be sung secretly

Before our retreat from Zhangjiakou, I had been working in the resource office of Mon-Jiang Bank. I was emotionally unhappy with the job. I had come to the Communist liberated area to do "revolution". Why then did I have to do ordinary clerical job? At the time, a party organization cadre told me, "The revolution asks you to do whatever, you do it. It does not matter even if it means sweeping the floor or cleaning the ditches..." Then, I somewhat came to understand what was meant by the concrete revolutionary work. During the march following the retreat from Zhangjiakou, I was a member of the bank's escorting team. I accompanied Captain Chen in his task to lead the transport team of over two hundred donkeys transporting toward Fuping the bank's gold, silver dollars and documents and archival files. Along the way, we from time to time encountered the advance units of the KMT army. I thus fully tasted the danger of guerilla war. There were times when both sides occupied the opposite corners of a village. After dusk, gun fire sounds arose. At times, surprised encounter with the enemy compelled us to dig trenches and started shooting. Sometimes we fired the shot to deceive the enemy.

When passing through a village, Communist troops would order the villagers to allow the soldiers to stay in their houses. During the night of their stay in the village, Communist authorities would mobilize the soldiers to watch villagers' struggling against and beating landlords, rich farmers or KMT members. Or, they were asked to take part in the people's trial. The soldiers were asked to learn "The class hatred the poor peasants have toward the landlords." However, as time went on, the soldiers were unhappy with their superiors for their discriminatory treatment. The superiors gave party members special care, but looked down on non-party members. When party members were sick, they got to visit doctors immediately, but others were, at best, provided a few more eggs to eat or told to rest a bit more.

New students from KMT-controlled area were even interfered for singing popular songs. If one was not careful, he could be criticized. In the 1930's, Communist Party's cultural work cadre Zhou Yang, who later served as head of Propaganda Department of CCP Central, proposed the so-called "Literature of National Defense", and attacked the works of democratic authors such as Lu Xun. Even anti-feudal works of Ba Jin were prohibited in the liberated area. Young people from Central and South China all liked to sing popular songs of the time. However, they had to sing quietly and secretly such songs of writers criticized by the Communists. I too liked one particular democratic song titled "The Depths of the Song" and learned to sing quietly with the young people.

The Depths of the Song

Fireflies fly in the empty courtyard, raccoons and
*   weasels walk on the platform, and I am accompanied*
*   by a lone lantern.*
The watchman rattles in the depth of the night. The
*   wind blows, the rain falls, flowers wither and leaves*
*   scatter around.*
In the long dark night, who is to keep me companied till
*   dawn? Who is to keep me companied to dawn?*
I might look likes a ferocious ghost but my heart is
*   steadfast and faithful, and as long as I breathe I am*

ready to battle the feudalistic fiend.

Ah, my lady, only with your eyes can see through the life of me.

Only with your heart can understand me.

You are a moon in the sky. I am the lone star on the edge of the moon.

You are a tree on the hill. I am the vine on the tree.

You are a pool of pure water. I am the water duckweed.

My lady, I would like to be in the grave taking vanity with me.

I am willing to emulate the exiled court historians writing all grievances of the earth.

Ah, lady, in this sea of darkness how do I express my anger but roll out my galloping waves of thoughts and write.

How do I want to comfort you, the lonely one?

Only the depths of the song, the depths of the song.

(Translated by Hou, Ping-Wen)

I remembered a song that the CCP members openly sang was titled "The East is Red" which glorified Mao Zedong. As for dances and theaters, there was the "Niu Yangge" (a folk dance of the Northwest) daily performed by all. And, the "White Haired Girl" was repeatedly performed by cultural work teams of the military, village or agricultural association. The CCP would focus on a thing while incessantly and repeatedly using the same way to express it. All would become tired of it, but the party would still not let go of it. Even though most of us could not tolerate it, but we would still outwardly pretend to applaud the performance. It was the same with meetings. The higher cadre of the Central Bureau had to talk about something repeatedly. People such as Zhou Yang, head of the Central Bureau Propaganda Department, and Chen Fanwu, president of the United University, and others had heavy accent of their own local dialects. It was difficult to understand the content of their speeches. We had to wait till the next day to read the "Liberation Daily" to know that they talked about.

Proposal for Organizing Taiwanese Corps

After Chiang Kaishek's KMT occupied Taiwan, the authorities seized over ten thousand Taiwanese soldiers from Hsinchu, Maoli, Chiayi, Taitung and other counties in Taiwan. These soldiers were organized into the "Newly-formed 70th Division" with Chen Yuanding, a lieutenant general from Northeast who graduated from the third class of the Huangpu Military Academy. Toward the end of 1946, Chiang Kaishek dispatched this newly-formed Taiwanese division to southwest Shantung Province along the Yellow River to fight in the Civil War against the Communists. In their very first encounter with the enemy, they not only lost the battle but were nearly demolished at Xuzhou. In May

1947, the Communist Eighth Route Army was renamed "People's Liberation Army". In the evening of June 30, 1947, Liu Bochen and Deng Xiaoping led 130,000 troops from Linxian of Shantung Province and marched over 300 li (Chinese miles) to Zhangqzheng to cross the Yellow River. The large army led by Liu and Deng dealt the KMT a crushing defeat at the Luxi (Western Shantung) Battle. The KMT 70th Division, formerly the Newly-formed 70th Division, was crushed and nearly 10,000 Taiwanese soldiers were captured.

In June 1948, 800,000 KMT troops and 600,000 People's Liberation troops met at Xuzhou to battle it out. The KMT army units were defeated one by one. With each defeat, 50,000 to 100,000 KMT men would be captured. And the army corps led by Huang Baitao was annihilated. In November, 1948, at Huaihai Campaign, which the KMT called Xuban Battle, Chiang Kaishek's KMT army was badly defeated. The military corps led by Huang Wei was annihilated, and Deputy Commander-In-Chief Du Yuming was captured while only Qiu Qingquan, the commander of the mechanical corps, committed suicide in front of the enemy. Therefore, Chiang Kaishek's war plan announced in early June, 1946 that he would defeat the main force of the People's Liberation Army within 6 months came to nothing.

More than 10,000 Taiwanese troops were captured by the Communist army led by Liu and Deng. Due to the fact that these young Taiwanese had received

Japanese military training, the Chinese Communists ordered them to take off KMT military uniforms and put on Communist ones and then had them sent back to the war front to fight the KMT troops. Being brave and good at fighting, the Taiwanese soldiers came straight at the enemy and consequently suffered heavy casualties.

From the "Liberation Daily", I learned that each report indicated two hundreds to three hundreds of Taiwanese casualties. My heart ached. First, they were captured for fighting against the Communists, and then they sacrificed their lives in fighting against the KMT troops. That was the saddest thing in the world. I hated the evil of alien rule. After much pondering, I thought of utilizing the development of the time to raise the issue of the Taiwanese soldiers so as to be helpful to them. I hastily proposed to the director of the Political Department of the Military Cadre School Wu Xi, (who was from Guangxi and a loyal and sincere veteran Communist cadre), that "The People's Liberation Army has successfully advanced against the KMT-controlled area. We will for sure conquer the entire China in no time. And before long it is inevitable that Chiang Kaishek would flee to Taiwan. Therefore, it is important that we do not allow the nearly 10,000 Taiwanese soldiers to be consumed at the battle front. They must be pulled back to the rear and given political training. When the time comes, they can return to Taiwan to do revolutionary work. It will be advantageous to the revolution."

Wu Xi and other school cadres were shocked by my unexpected prediction of an event to come. They must have immediately reported to authorities at Yanan. Within a month, the Party Central in Yanan telegraphed to call me to go from Fuping (in Jun-Cha-Ji Military Region headquarters) to Chun-Ji-Lu(Shantung)-Yu(Honan). The commander of Jun-Ji-Lu-Yu was Liu Bochen while its political commissar was Deng Xiaoping. On March 8, 1947, at Fuping's Central Bureau guesthouse, I read a "Liberation Daily" report on the explosive happening of Taiwan's February 28 Great Revolution. I was emotionally stirred. However, Chinese always manufactured history. For example, in 1975, Liao Chenchi insisted, "The 228 Great Revolution is part of the Chinese Revolution led by Mao Zedong and the CCP."

In March, 1947, Hilaka and I each carried a comforter and our daily supplies. Accompanied by a little fellow/guard and under his watchful eyes, we walked for over 40 days passing through a good number of towns to finally arrive at the headquarters of Jun-Ji-Lu-Yu Military Region. We stayed in the guesthouse at Niutoucun. During our trip, at each and every village, big and small, we bumped into tragic bloody struggle of land reform. Landlords were slowly put to death while their dependents were banished from their village that they got quite ill along the road. In addition, the KMT was already invading or occupying neighboring villages. With mixed feelings, for over a month I didn't have any desire to appreciate the scenery along the way.

In April of the same year (1947), an Organization Department senior cadre, who was of low cultural level but was serious and honest, came to inform me that my superiors want me to organize a "Taiwan Unit." Before long, Political Commissar (a Sicuan man) and his subordinate Zhang (an honest party member from Guangdong) transferred to me over 200 Taiwanese soldiers from the 7th Brigade of the original Liu-Deng Army. The Party Central also decided within a year to transfer to me 5,000 Taiwanese soldiers for training. As I was not a party member, I did not have the official title of captain.

The majority of the Taiwanese soldiers were less than twenty years old. After arriving in China mainland, they didn't know the Chinese people and their country, did not speak Chinese languages and were un-accustomed to life in China. Among them, there was circulated saying such as "Eating millet rice, one expels yellow excrement. To expel white one, let's hurry back to Taiwan (to eat white rice)." I was worried. In order to ease the depression of my fellow Taiwanese, I took them to fish in the nearby streams. (In North China plains, fish in the ponds had high content of salt and thus were not edible. As for soft-shelled turtles, due to their awful nickname, they were not considered desirable either.) As a result, psychologically the young

Taiwanese felt a little better.

In July of the same year (1947), the authorities transferred to lead the Taiwan Unit Cai Gongqiu (who was a Hakha from Meixian, Guangdong, a party member and previously with LiangGuang Brigade) while I Lin Tou was formally made a political teacher. Toward the end of July, Taiwan Unit departed from the guesthouse of Jun-Ji-Lu-Yu military headquarters. After marching for 3 days and 2 nights, we arrived at Lierzhuang, Nangonxian, Hobei Province (which was the castle of the favorite concubine of Shang Dynasty King Zhou in the 9th century before Christ). It was there that "Taiwan Unit of Jun-Ji-Lu-Yu Military Region" was officially formed. The organization and structure of the Unit as follows:

Captain: Cai Gongqiu

Political officer: Lin Shijun (a Hainan Islander, party member, Yanan Resist-Japan University graduate, Hainan Island dialect was close to Taiwanese)

Political teacher: Lin Tuo (Su Beng had never joined CCP even though repeatedly asked to join the party. Su Beng used not having sufficiently learned as the excuse.)

Political teacher: Xin Qiao (a man from Jilin, Northeast, understood Japanese and was appointed as a political teacher to covertly listen to talks among Taiwanese soldiers. I understood that he was a KMT member when in Shenyang. Later, he went to Yanan to study at Resist-Japan University. Ultimately, he committed suicide in Beijing.)

By June, 1948, the "People's Liberation Army" of the CCP had completely mopped KMT troops from Northeast and North China, except Beijing, Tianjin, Taiyuan, Qingdao and a few other small places. The CCP Central combined Jun-Cha-Ji and Jun-Ji-Lu-Yu military regions into "North China Military Region". The Central Bureau's First Secretary was Liu Shaoqi, Second Secretary Bo Yipo, and Third Secretary Nie Rongchen while Military Region Commander was Nie Rongchen, Political Commissar Bo Yipo, First Deputy Commander Xu Xiangqian, Second Deputy Commander Teng Daiyuan and Third Deputy Commander Xiao Ke.

In April of the same year (1948), Mao Zedong, Chu De, Liu Shaoqi, Zhou Enlai, Ren Mishi and other party leading cadres had moved from Yannan to North China Military Region. Mao lived in Xibonan Village in the northwestern corner of Shijiazhuang. During the First Civil War (1927-36), Chinese Communists established "Red Army University" at Jinggangshan while they next set up "Resist-Japan University" at Yanan during the Resistance War (1937-45). Now they combined the two universities and named it "North China Military and Political University". Chief of Staff of North China

Military Region Yeh Jianying simultaneously served as the university president and political commissar while Xiao Ke vice president and vice political commissar and Teng Daiyuan vice president and vice political commissar.

Taiwan Unit subsequently moved from Lierzhuang to Shijiazhuang taking position at the former Japanese military camp there. It became the First Battalion of "North China Military and Political University's Cadre Corps" and directly came under the university's leadership. The Unit's Captain was Cai Gonqiiu, Vice-captain Liao Xianjing (Yangmei, Hsinchu, party member, made meritorious contribution on the battle front and was considered a principal hero, but was a flatterer), Political Commissar Yang Chen (Taiwanese born in Indonesia, party member, Xiamen Jimai Middle School graduate, Resist-Japan University graduate, worked at Central Youth Training Class, allegedly he was killed by Red Guards). Political Commissar Lin Shijun, Vice-Captain and Vice-Political-Commissar Zhang Shenwu (Lierzhuang Village Chief and Secretary, typical party bureaucrat, local tyrant, and allegedly in 1957 he directed the struggle against Xie Xuehong from behind the scenes), Political Officer Xin Qiao, Political Officer Lin Tuo. Later, from United University the authorities transferred to Taiwan Unit Education officer Liu Shiying (of Gansan, Taiwan, party member), Education Officer Lin Hanzhang (of Yilan, Taiwan, party member), and Education Officer Zhang Wenhua (of

Tainan, Taiwan, party member). As a result, among all Taiwan Unit cadres, I Lin Tuo was the only non-party member.

In this way, Taiwan Unit and the life of every Taiwanese all came under and controlled by local tyrants and dictatorial party bureaucrats who ignored humanity and were sinister and evil.

On the other hand, the young Taiwanese were really good for nothing. Once suppressed by CCP, they competed to become party members. Divided into factions and engaged in in-fighting, they beat to death one man from Chiayi.

People's Trials and Hell on Earth

Since the 1930's, the Chinese Communists had decided on "Rural Policy", each village had CCP branch. Serving simultaneously as the village chief, the village branch clerk was the one and only dictator of the village. He controlled the armed militia. He had villagers help till his land. Having the village government under his control and acting arrogantly, he was denigrated as "rural tyrant/emperor".

Along the way, during our retreat from Zhangjiakou, I saw heads of Buddha statues knocked off everywhere. To my question why, the party cadres answered, "The ordinary village folks have become ideologically progressive. They consider religions to be opium and therefore they took it on themselves to remove the Buddha's heads." Once we arrived in a village, the cadre in charge would assign workers to stay in villagers' houses. I developed friendly relations with the villagers with whom I stayed. I often helped them carry water and did their chores. They all took me as Japanese. The people I met all belonged to the poorest and lowest social classes. However, almost without exceptions, they were honest and authentically fine Chinese.

One night, when I came out to the yard to pee, I found the family members worshiping Heavenly Lord while kneeling on the ground and with incense sticks in their hands. I was greatly surprised as were they. I asked, "When you have chopped off heads of Buddha statues in the temples, why are you worshipping now?" They answered, "That resulted from our being forced by the Communist Party." I was greatly shocked by such an answer. That night I could hardly sleep. I asked myself, "Marxism does not have this. Doesn't Marxism talk about restoring humanity? Why does it change to such extent? What should I be doing here (in China)? I a Taiwanese should be doing what kind of revolutionary work?" For several days, I felt as if I had lost my spirit and soul. Until then, I had been able to walk 50 to 60 li a day, but I could not even finish half of the distance. I talked to myself, "I cannot continue like this." As a result, I had greater doubt about the methods and measures of the Chinese Communists.

During its two thousand years of feudal imperial

system, the Chinese society had never had revolution that changed its fundamental system. (There were only changes of dynastic names, but not revolution for two thousand years.) Under the semi-colonial landlord system since the late Qing period, the peasant masses lived in extreme poverty. In the cold winter of North China, I noticed that the young couple who lived across from my place. When the husband went outside, his wife always stayed indoors. On the other hand, when the wife left her house, her husband always stayed home. Later I asked others for explanation, I was told that they were so poor that they had only one pair of heavy pants to share. The great majority of folks drank millet rice porridge and chewed buns, but rarely had noodles. The best side dishes they could afford were occasional tofu and white cabbage.

In 1946, the Chinese Communists promulgated their policy of "land reform" and started land reform struggles. Its ultimate goal was not only to distribute land to landless peasants, but also through using un-humane struggle method to quickly eliminate social classes as well as physical bodies of landlords, rich peasants and KMT members. Whenever each and every village carried out land reform, the Party's Central Bureau dispatched a team of supervisors to the village to instruct villagers the model method of bloody struggle. What we saw was in the day time landlords and rich peasants had to work in the field while at night they would be struggled against. They, male and female, were all hung up and beaten with sticks. They were ordered to tell concrete cases of their exploiting tenants and poor peasants. They had to tell where they had hidden their gold bars and silver dollars. After repeated beatings, they bled and their skins shred. Only then the so-called "People's Court" began the trial.

The people's referees set up ahead of time the rack from which the struggled subjects would be hung upside down. To the right of the rack was a spiritual table on it placed the spiritual tablets of the tenants' parents. Kitchen knives, scissors, knives for butchering cows and sheep and sticks were placed on the table to the left of the rack. Then the beating of drums and gongs mobilized villagers, male and female of all ages, to come attending the meeting. There was a fine of two jin (Chinese pounds) of sesame oil for everyone who failed to show up. For the impoverished villagers, when even an egg was treasured, they could not afford to pay two jins of sesame oil. Consequently, they one by one slowly showed up at the square to attend the trial.

At one people's trial, I witnessed a landlord hung from the rack was struggled for several days and beaten badly. This landlord was a 70-year-old woman with bound feet. The man in charge of the trial was a party branch secretary and village chief. From the beginning, he loudly shouted to the tenants saying, "Your parents suffered much mistreatments from her father and you yourself also have been exploited by her all your life. Now that you are masters, your time to express your bitterness and take revenge has come..." At the same time, party members and militiamen, who were planted among the over 200 villagers, shouted noisily. They helped to put pressure on the folks involved. Under such highly inflamed atmosphere, the tenants were both surprised and fearful. Crying and praying, they bowed and knelt on the ground in front of their parents' spiritual tables. The trial leader took over again and loudly detailed how the landlord harshly exploited petty tenants. Finally, he asked, "How should we punish this evil, reactionary landlord?" Every militia man present raised his gun shouted, "Shot her! Shot her!" There were, however, some who shouted, "That's not enough. Not enough!" Militiamen followed by shouting, "It's not acceptable unless she is sliced with knives till her death!" At long last, the trial leader said, "Those of you who opposed the move raise your hands." Under the situation, who dared to raise his/her hands. This constituted "the decision of the people." Again, the trial leader said to all who were present, "Each and every one of you must use a knife to stab her or a stick to beat her, ok?" Militiamen shouted collectively, "Yes! Yes! It's decided! It's decided!"

However, who was to be the first one to lay a knife on the landlord? The majority of the villages had close relations and all wanted to avoid that horrible chore. Therefore, it was decided by lot. A man unfortunately was drawn to be the first to pick a weapon to use against the female landlord. Nevertheless, not being able to bring himself to do it, he knelt dis-spiritedly in the center of the square. Then, the trial leader through the woman's association compelled the man's wife to curse him. Faced with no alternatives, the wife cursed her husband for lacking courage and for being counter-revolutionary. She shouted, "Do you want to oppose the Communist Party and go against the people's judgment? If so, I want to divorce you. It's better you die." She wept and cried. While cursing, she used her fist to hit her husband's head and kicked his back, etc. She wanted him to kill the landlord who had done wrongs to the people. In the meantime, the militiamen began screaming loudly. The entire square came under the violent atmosphere that greatly stirred up much restlessness among the folks.

Under much pressure, the guy suddenly stood up to seize a stick from the table next to him. Moving close to the female landlord, he hastily and in panic-like swung the stick at the side of her head. With one single blow, there was only one sound of "Yia" from the landlord and her skull was broken. Blood and white brain flew out of her head. It was like hell on earth. Then the second person, the third... followed. Beating and killing became easier for those who followed. Some used butcher's knife to stab, some used a pair of scissors to cut while some others used a ball bat. Some cut at her ears, or nose, and so on and so forth.

Most of the villagers closed their eyes for they dared not look directly at the hellish scene. Again, I suffered serious shock. The Communist Party that claimed to be a socialist revolutionary organization actually appeared as the hideous and ferocious executioner.

That day I could not eat and sleep. The 4 members of the family, with them I stayed, did not eat either and remained extremely quiet. The whole day I lay down in the kang bed. I talked to myself, "Marxism does not have this awful stuff. Does not Marxism talk about destroying social classes in order to restore humanity? How could it transform into such a tragic world? What am I supposed to do here? I cannot continue on like this. I have to do revolution of liberation that is different from this." While talking to myself, I thought of Taiwan and felt homesick.

What is the so-called "Mao Zedong Thought"? One day while traveling, I suddenly recalled a poem of Mao titled "SNOW --to the tune of Chin Yuan Chun".

SNOW
--to the tune of Chin Yuan Chun

North country scene:
A hundred leagues locked in ice,
A thousand leagues of whirling snow.
Both sides of the Great Wall
One single white immensity.
The Yellow River's swift current

Is stilled from end to end.
The mountains dance like silver snakes
And the highlands charge like wax-hued elephants,
Vying with heaven in stature.
On a fine day, the land,
Clad in white, adorned in red,
Grows more enchanting.

This land so rich in beauty
Has made countless heroes bow in homage.
But alas! Chin Shih-huang and Han Wu-ti
Were lacking in literary grace,
And Tang Tai-tsung and Sung Tai-tsu
Had little poetry in their souls;
And Genghis Khan,
Proud Son of Heaven for a day,
Knew only shooting eagles, bow outstretched
All are past and gone!
For truly great men
Look to this age alone.

Mao composed the essay in the winter of 1935 when he was 43 years of age. He was then leading the Red Army on the Long March to cross mountains and rivers. And, after having crossed many mountains and rivers and experienced icy sky and snow-covered land and other hardships, he and his followers finally arrived in Yannan. He was a sentimental man and a romantic poet who possessed limitless elegant terms and phrases as well as writing skills. This poem, however, also revealed his dream. He dreamed of being an emperor of the past. In his consciousness he could not let go of the imperial idea of the feudal era. If Mao Zedong was really the great teacher of the people, then he should have stood on the side of the laboring masses. What should have been in his heart and mind should be stories that common folks had widely and fondly recited. For example, the story of Lady Meng who cried to death at the foot of the Great Wall where her husband had perished as one of the tens and thousands of workers conscripted by the First Emperor to build the Great Wall. I did visit the well-known Shanhaiguan, a Great Wall gate located where mountain and sea meets. And, I visited the Temple that worshipped Lady Meng.

To sum up, the Mao Zedong Thought is nothing but a combination of Chinese imperial thought and Stalin's idea of dictatorship. Mao's individual totalitarian dictatorship was far worse than that of the various emperors of the past. Mao considered himself to be sacred and inviolable. More so than any Chinese emperors, Mao believed that he could do no wrongs. Such view contradicts the socialist principle of ending oppressions of hierarchical social classes.

The One Party Dictatorship of the Chinese Communist Party

(1) Marxism

"Manifesto of the Communist Party"

In order to restore "humanity", Marx and Engels (who thought that under capitalism humanity would be lost), in their "Manifesto of the Communist Party" (1848), used the scientific method to establish "Marxism" (which focuses on reform of social system, explains that capitalism will inevitably collapse and that Communism will eventually be established) and resorted to proletarian revolution to carry out Communism.

The "First International": 1864-76, various left-wing revolutionary organizations of Western Europe jointly formed the International Workers' Association to work on the liberation of proletarian classes.

The "Second International": 1889-1914, brought together workers of the world, and hoped to struggle for political power in various countries through the effort of socialist parties.

During the First World War (1914-18), workers of various countries chose to protect and defend their "fatherland", and avoided taking "class line".

The Second International split into 2:

(1) The route of "Socialist Democracy": In terms of the socialist method for the liberation of proletarian class, it excluded proletarian dictatorship, and firmly set on utilizing the parliamentary system to realize socialist ideal of "from each according to his ability and to each according to his contribution."

(2)The route of "Leninist": 1917-24, which resorted to armed revolution to achieve Communism of "from each according to one's ability and to each according to one's needs."

The "Third International": Lenin advocated the use of arms to solve national problems and agricultural problems and to bring down Capitalism so as to achieve Communism.

"Stalin's violent, one-man dictatorship": 1928-53. After Lenin's death in 1924, Stalin continued Lenin's violent revolution. He then developed without restraints his individual tyranny, one-party dictatorship and Communist Imperialism. Later, according to records, Stalin killed 40,000,000 to 50,000,000 Soviet citizens.

"Maoism": After Mao Zedong became the chairman of the CCP, he combined Chinese feudalistic imperialist ideology with modern (Fascist) violence of Stalinism and implemented One-party individual dictatorship in China. It is estimated that from 1945-76 more than 40,000,000 Chinese were killed.

(2) Chinese Communist Party ("CCP" in short)

"Party Members": In 2007, they totaled

73,360,000. Party members must absolutely obey the Party's leadership.

"Party Branches": The entire country has 3,200,000 party branches. A party branch consists of more than 3 members. A village has a party branch while a street committee of residents constitutes a branch. A branch exists in each and every organization, public or private, school, media, enterprise, etc. Party committee officers appoint branch secretaries.

"Party Committee Members": Party committee is the superior organization to party branches. It receives orders from the Party's Central Committee and leads party branches under its jurisdiction. Committee members are appointed by the Political Bureau of the Central Committee.

"National Congress of Party Representatives": On the surface, it is the "Supreme Organ of Party Authority", but in reality it has over 2,000 local representatives. All of them are internally appointed by the Political Bureau of the Central Committee. This fictional body meets once every five years.

"Central Committee of the Party": Formally, the National Congress of Party Representatives elects people to constitute the party's highest leadership organization. In reality, it has over 200 Central Committee members who are internally appointed by the Political Bureau of the Central Committee.

"Political Bureau of the Central Committee": When the Central Committee is in recess, the Bureau carries out the functions of the Central Committee. In reality, the over 20 members of the Bureau are internally appointed by the general secretary of the Party.

"Standing Committee of the Political Bureau": Formally, members of the Standing Committee are elected from among members of the Political Bureau. In reality, the 9 members of the Standing Committee are appointed by the general secretary of the Party.

"General Secretary (Chairman) of the Party": Formally, he is elected by members of the Standing Committee of the Political Bureau. But in reality, he is designated by the previous general secretary. Thus, Deng Xiaoping designated Jiang Zemin while Jiang Zemin designated Hu Jintao.

In the structural system of the CCP as described above, the general secretary of the Party and members of the Standing Committee of the Political Bureau necessarily become the supreme dictators. Collectively they hold absolute power over the party, government, military and police to become one-party dictatorship.

(3) The People's Republic of China (in short PRC)

One-party Dictatorship of CCP

The CCP is the only political party in the PRC. The many parties of the so-called "Political Consultative Conference" are wall-flower parties that are manufactured by the CCP. As a result, political power is exercised by CCP in the fashion of one-party dictatorship.

"People's National Congress of Representatives": Formally, this is the assembly of representatives elected by the people. In reality, the great majority (90%) of the representatives are party members appointed by the Political Bureau.

Executive Power: The Chairman of the ROC government is the Generl Secretary of the Party. Premier, ministers, and senior officers of all central and local governments must be party members. All central and local government units must have party committee and its members exercise personnel and financial power and authority. The bureaucratic system is entirely in step with the party system. The CCP controls the executive power.

Judicial Power: Like executive power, judicial power is in the hands of the CCP. All prosecutorial organs, public security police and trial courts of central and local level are served by party members and controlled by the party organization.

People's Liberation Army: Led and directed by the party's Central Military Affairs Committee. The party's general secretary serves as the chairman of the Committee. As a result, the commander-in-chief of the army is the general secretary of the party. All military men must be party members. As a result, the army is a party army and not national army. While in the Republic of China Chiang Kaishek's dictatorship is horrible, Mao Zedong's one-party supremacy in the PRC is several times worse.

Therefore, through the party organization the CCP completely controls the executive power, judicial power, military and police and other political power. It practices one-party dictatorship of political domination.

Stalin died in 1953 while Mao Zedong's death came in 1976. In 1990 came the collapse of both the government of and the Communist Party of the Soviet Union. Thereafter, the original Marxism has suffered fatal impact. However, the world's communist countries are individually still under the Stalinist one-party dictatorship political system.

On the other hand, after the First World War, social democratic revolutions have developed. In Germany, Scandinavian countries, or English-speaking countries, the liberal democratic system has prevailed. Socialism differs from Communism.

During the Cold War between the United States and Soviet Union, the East and the West opposed each other. In theory and system, it is Capitalism vs. Stalinist Communism. It is also free world vs. un-free world and democracy vs. dictatorship (Fascism).

2.
中國「少數民族」的獨立運動

（一）「中華思想」是民族矛盾的濫觴

中國新疆省維吾爾（Uighur）自治區烏魯木齊（Wūlǔmùgi）市政府，在二〇〇九年七月六日，宣稱：「五日夜發生維吾爾族人暴動，死亡一四〇人，負傷八二六人。」（日本記者野口東秀，由烏魯木齊電告產經新聞）

「維吾爾人蜂起，飛速發展於同一自治區的喀什（Kashgar）。」（AP通信，美國通信）

在中國史上，大小民族的對立矛盾，是所謂「社會動亂」的火藥庫，其根源，一貫是在漢族對他族所採取的優越與差別。

中國漢族定住於黃河下流地域，從古就誇稱自己為華夏·中華·中原，對周遭的其他族群，反卻以低賤的番族叫稱，即東夷·北狄·南蠻·西戎（古代的匈奴·鮮卑·羯·氐·羌等族），而把其卑視·睥睨在其威壓之下。

這種優越與差別之名稱，均內涵著：「漢族文化·生活都高於其他異族」、「中華是世界上最高峰的地理中心」、

「中原帝王君臨世界」、「華夏帝王受異族朝貢」等漢族至尊的優越思想。這稱之爲「中華思想」（Sino-Centrism）。

中華思想在史上，再發展爲漢族帝國干犯緣邊異族的「五服制」。「古代王畿外圍地域，以五百里爲率，視距離遠近分爲五等，即甸服‧侯服‧綏服‧要服‧荒服。」（尚書‧禹貢）若有傷害中華至尊或危及其霸權，立即興兵問罪。

台灣古來被稱爲「荒服地」（清‧劉良璧「台灣府志」），被認爲是距離中華最遠的化外異地。

公元十八世紀，西力東漸後，近代的西歐帝國民族主義概念，打垮封建的中華思想，才遽變以「大漢沙文主義」（Han Chauvinism）爲禍胎的「中華民族主義」。

中華民族主義，在反帝反封建及抗日戰時，固然是解放的‧革命的。然而第二次世界大戰終結後，遽然再急轉直下成爲侵略‧反動的帝國殖民主義，蔣家中國國民黨中華民國即以侵略並殖民統治台灣（1945），中國共產黨中華人民共和國（1949），則以抑壓‧屠殺中國的弱小民族，及叫囂要武力進攻台灣。

(二)「中華民族」概念的虛構性

中國共產黨，即以佔人口絕大多數的漢民族爲政治統治基礎，實行一黨專政，並徹底利用漢民族的「中華民族主義」，把居住中國領土的大小民族，虛構的（false）編爲中

華民族的一員。

實際上，現在中國，惟有漢民族才能稱得起是中華民族，其他五十五個弱小民族，毫無例外的均擁有單一性（unify）與主體性（identity）的社會集團。故不能被包括在中華民族的範疇（希臘Kategoria, 英category）之內。在中國史上，何時何地都沒有這種「中華民族」的存在（羅馬esse, 英being, 德Sein, 法être）。現在中國也不可能有這種中華民族的存在。這種包括許多單一民族的中華民族，不過是從政治目的造成出來的一種虛構的民族概念（羅馬conceptio, 英・法concept, 德Begriff）（日本・中國問題評論專家，中國・四川出身人，歸化日本，石平「これが本当の中国の33のつぼ」這就是中國眞正的33個問題的焦點，2008）。

（三）中國政府及漢民族壓制國內其他弱小民族

中國的總人口，現在約有十三、四億人（2007年數字），分為五十六個單一民族。其中，漢民族人口佔總人口的絕大多數，九一・六％，十一億五千九四〇萬人。

人口少數的五十五個小民族，主要的有：壯民族（人口一六一八萬人，住廣西自治區），回民族（人口九八二萬人，住寧夏自治區），維吾爾民族（人口八四〇萬人，住新疆自治區），蒙古民族（人口五八一萬人，住內蒙古自治區），西藏民族（人口五四二萬人，住西藏自治區）等。

　　但是從一九四九年中國共產黨取得中國政權以來，一貫以恐嚇政治手段對弱小少數民族的同化政策，對全國異民族的自治區進行滲透性漢族移民政策，結果，蒙古自治區的漢人人口已佔蒙古自治區全人口的八二％，維吾爾自治區漢人人口佔四三％，西藏自治區漢人人口超過五○％（2008年統計數字），弱小民族的傳統‧文化以及生活均遭破壞，以致能講母語的弱小民族，逐步減少。

　　壯‧回‧維‧蒙‧西藏等五十五民族，有史以來就居住於中國王權的行政區域之外，各族都有個別的居住地域，各有各的歷史‧文化‧語言或文字，而且擁有自己的領土與政府，所以不管人口多數或少數，從歷史觀點或社會概念來說，他們都擁有與漢民族完全不同的一個民族存在。然而因中央亞細亞與中國的歷史過程，他們現在才居住於漢民族為中心的中華人民共和國版圖之內。

　　中國共產黨中華人民共和國，把這五十五個異民族置於政治統治之下，並以漢民族為主體，卑稱這些五十五民族為「少數民族」（national minorities, minority race）。

　　中國政府，雖然把這些異民族的居住地域，行政上使用「自治區」的名稱，在實質上，這些自治區的最高權力者，毫無例外的皆由中國共產黨「區黨委」漢人書記所佔，是絕不允許異民族行使自治權，或主張獨立權，而是加以無底洞的壓制與殘殺。

（四）中國弱小民族的獨立運動

一九四九年中國共產黨取得中國天下，中國弱小民族才一律受到近代的‧有組織的政治侵佔，即：漢人移民浸透‧民族差別深化‧宗教彈壓熾烈‧文化破壞徹底‧壓殺獨立運動，以及資本侵略與經濟掠奪等等，所以無論大小的諸異族都起來反抗，企圖脫離中國，而達成民族獨立。

特別是新疆的維吾爾民族與西藏民族，因各有伊斯蘭教（Islam）與西藏喇嘛教（Tibet Lamaism）為精神支柱，所以對抗共黨政府及漢人的獨立運動頻仍發生。

中國政府對異族的壓殺，開始於一九五七年的「反右派鬥爭」，許許多多的蒙古‧維吾爾‧西藏等異族黨幹部，都被淘汰（此時，以地方民族主義為名，海南島的馮白駒等抗日領袖遭慘殺，台灣的謝雪紅‧江文也被清算）。

西藏民族從一九五九年開始，遭共黨機械化大軍入侵，而掀起全西藏第一次大反抗，西藏佛教法王（也是西藏族政治領導人）達賴‧喇嘛等僧侶與獨立人士，成群越過喜瑪拉雅山脈，逃亡印度，在印度西北部樹立了亡命獨立政府（參加的西藏人據聞有十幾萬人）。達賴‧喇嘛屢次要求共黨政府一起舉行和談，期以實現「自治」，但是共黨政府不但不應自治，而且在西藏內部進行大屠殺。一九八七、八九年，共黨西藏地區黨委書記胡錦濤（現任中共中央黨總書記），指揮大軍進行大彈壓大屠殺。雖然遭到這種非人道的大彈壓，然西藏族人要求民族獨立的抗爭不但未遭毀滅，且更加強盛熾

烈。

　　滿清朝廷曾在十八世紀中葉，侵佔距北京三千餘公里的西北角，東突厥斯坦（Eastern Turkistan），這因被認爲是新的中國領土，故名稱「新疆」。新疆擁有一六六萬平方公里面積，佔全中國六分之一的領土。

　　新疆在滿清時代，即以伊斯蘭教徒維吾爾人崛起，宣告「東突厥斯坦運動」（突厥斯坦屬於土耳其族人住地，今維吾爾自治區），一九三三年興起第一次獨立運動，宣言「東突厥斯坦伊斯蘭共和國」，一九四四年第二次獨立運動時也宣言「東突厥斯坦共和國」，但均遭鎮壓，然而維吾爾獨立運動其後也繼續不斷的發生。

　　共黨中國政府於一九四九年設立維吾爾自治區，是維吾爾族·回族·哈薩克族等弱小民族的共住地，然共產政府入侵後，漢族人大規模的被送入該自治地區，使漢族人在自治區佔最大人口勢力。同時，共黨政府派遣毛澤東左右手的大將王震，率領「新疆建設兵團」（下設十四個兵團，十萬大軍，裝甲兵團·砲兵團，以及三萬武裝警察，以隔絕漢維兩族關係，鎮壓反抗，駐防屯墾等爲任務）。如一九九〇年維吾爾獨立運動興起「東突厥斯坦伊斯蘭運動」，立即遭北京直接指揮的新疆建設兵團的武裝大兵所鎮壓。「一九九七年六月，烏魯木齊的維吾爾族人一萬五千，以木棒·石器等蜂擁而起，結果，二百餘維吾爾住民遭屠殺，六千人被送入勞動營，一九四九年至七二年，記錄著反共黨政府的蜂起共有五四八件，三十六萬維吾爾族人被殺害。」（香港，Foreign Report，

2009/2/28）

　　維吾爾人的世界著名作家，阿部突烏爾灰骨證言，「維吾爾教師，幾乎遭新疆建設兵團武警捉去坐牢，僅只數年，被認為有獨立思想的維吾爾人遭到綁架，而永不能回家的有二十五萬人」（日本・產經新聞）。

　　這幾年，中國西北部頻頻發生弱小民族反中國政府事件，如在維吾爾自治區帕米爾高原（Pamir），維吾爾自治區西南部（天山南路）大城市喀什（Kashgar），從烏魯木齊飛往北京的客機上，雲南省昆明市內公車上，或青海省克爾庫等地，相繼發生反中國政府的爆炸事件。

（五）烏魯木齊維吾爾人蜂起

　　烏魯木齊是新疆維吾爾自治區首邑，天山北路的大都市（「絲路」上的一個綠洲oasis），古代駱駝商隊的貿易中心。

　　因廣東韶關一家玩具廠的二個維吾爾工人被漢人殺害，二〇〇九年七月五日夜，在烏魯木齊發生數千人維吾爾人蜂起抗議，官方宣佈死亡一四〇人，受傷八二八人。

　　當場目睹的日本旅行者說：「最初是維吾爾族人與漢族人互相破口罵街遊行，然而中國政府武裝部隊突然出現，向維吾爾人開槍，引起遊行群眾爆發憤懣，進而同族住民陸續捲入抗議行列，維漢互相打鬥・破壞對方的商店・住所等，遂成為刀・棒・石塊對機槍的大規模抗爭，眼看各處血跡斑斑，有如人間煉獄。」（日本・產經新聞）

　　北京政府，聞訊急遽派遣中國武警部隊（據稱有百萬人馬）司令員吳雙戰，及國家安全部長孟建柱趕至烏魯木齊，投入千餘武裝警察，軍隊・鎮暴車・戰車等，直接向維吾爾人開槍・施放催淚彈・水柱，或以電棒打人，其中更有鎮暴車直接衝入維吾爾人的遊行群眾中，十七人被壓在鎮暴車下當場死亡（AFP，法國通信）。

　　「武裝警察抓到遊行行列中的維吾爾人，將其身上衣物剝光，且推倒在地，穿軍靴的腳踩在頭顱及臉頰，然後當成暴民捉走，……數百維吾爾婦女，舉拳掩面泣訴，口口聲聲要求“還我丈夫”。」「維漢兩族均各自組織自衛隊，在大街上・小巷內到處大血戰。」（日本・產經新聞）

　　烏魯木齊市政府當局，七月七日在記者會上強調：「此次暴動不屬民族問題或宗教問題，而是亡命外國的維吾爾人，組織世界維吾爾會議，為了分裂祖國，有計劃並煽動的。此次暴動死亡一五六人。」

　　新疆埋藏石油・天然瓦斯等地下資源豐富（佔全中國的三〇％），並廣設有核能諸設施，所以共黨聲稱：「新疆是中國的生命線，是與維吾爾獨派打仗的最前線。」（日本・野口東秀記者，由烏魯木齊電告）

　　維吾爾族蜂起抗議，實以共黨政府利用漢族人的優越性實行抑壓統治為因，所以新疆・西藏等這種弱小民族對中國的民族產生反感，此後是更加深化對立，共黨政府的血腥彈壓政策也會更加殘酷。

　　共黨政府對於新疆自治區的交通等經濟基本建設，是從

一九九○年代開始，突飛猛進的發展，導致新疆的GDP年平均為一○％的成長。然而這些國營產業的高幹地位及巨大利益，完全由新移民的漢民族人所壟斷，而且，強制以中國話為普遍通用語言，弱小民族的母語‧文化‧宗教等盡遭干涉，所以維吾爾族人認為共黨與漢人是資源掠奪‧文化破壞‧毀滅民族的元凶，維吾爾獨立運動只要有機會就會爆發。
（維吾爾經濟學者談話──日本‧產經新聞）

　　共黨政府對外發表：「烏魯木齊暴動是海外的分裂勢力"世界維吾爾會議"所指揮的有計劃有組織的暴動」，但是，國際社會並不相信，大體上都認為這是為要執行恐怖與屠殺勾當的藉口。

　　國際特赦組織，呼籲中國政府立即釋放被捕維吾爾人。

　　聯合國秘書長潘基文聲明：「國內或國際上的不同意見，均應透過對話來和平解決。」

　　美國國務卿希拉蕊七日發言：「美國對此深感關切，將盡全力了解真相，……目前當務之急是設法結束衝突。」
（日本記者古森義久，由華盛頓報導）

　　然而，中國政府與維吾爾民族的衝突事件延及海外，中國駐荷蘭‧德國‧挪威‧日本等地大使館或領事館，均遭維吾爾族人及其國際朋友示威或攻擊，他們都高舉「中國人滾回中國」的旗幟。

　　中國國家主席胡錦濤（黨中央總書記），在義大利擬以舉行八國高峰會（G8），因新疆形勢告急，隨之取消行程，於七月八日搭乘專機返回北京，立即發表聲明：「世界維吾爾

會議議長熱比婭‧卡提爾爲暴動的主謀。」

　　被中國政府責難爲「煽動暴動的國家分離者」的熱比婭‧卡提爾（62歲），於七月二十八日，從美國訪問日本。她曾在中國因政治犯而坐牢六年，她丈夫坐牢九年，二人的孩子各被判七年與九年徒刑，兩人現仍在監獄服刑。她在二〇〇五年亡命美國，〇六年就任「世界維吾爾會議議長」，被稱爲「維吾爾之母」，諾貝爾和平獎候補。

　　她二十九日在東京，日本記者俱樂部會見內外記者（包含「人民日報」記者在內），她說：「烏魯木齊發生遊行運動以降，萬人單位的維吾爾人行方不明，中國政府的恐怖彈壓（terrorism）現仍繼續進行。」

　　「由中國共產黨侵略後，祖國東突厥斯坦被置於中國支配之下，約已六〇年，維吾爾人的和平的生活被剝奪，青年人不能住在故鄉，均爲服務都市的勞動而被捉走，若不去，馬上以反政府‧國家分裂主義者‧恐怖份子羅織罪名，維吾爾的語言‧文化‧宗教都被禁止或抹殺……」

　　「集結在烏魯木齊的維吾爾人的遊行，事前有發聲明，所以，中國當局的鎮壓措施也早有準備。維吾爾人與漢人互相攻擊因而造成死傷者眾的初期階段，武裝警察故意不出手干預，先將混亂的現場攝影後，目的是要當成維吾爾人的暴力行爲的證據而將之公諸於世。」

　　「到當晚九點，全市全面停電，在漆黑的暗夜裡，從數個地方同時響起猛烈的機關槍的槍聲，武裝警官的無差別攻擊開始。」

「但是一到翌日早上，維吾爾人的遺體都被清理乾淨，只獨留漢人死屍在現場的場面，以這樣的現場佈置企圖讓人誤認為是維吾爾人襲擊漢人，並發表犧牲者一九七人皆是漢人。」

「實際上，從中國政府的映像，可以看出手拿武器的都是漢人，維吾爾人是手無寸鐵，擺明就是"武裝漢人與武裝警察及軍隊"對待"手無寸鐵的維吾爾人"的情況下，有武裝的漢人能被無武裝的維吾爾人殺得那麼多？實際上，被殺的都是無武裝的維吾爾人，我們估計千人以上的維吾爾人被殺害。」

「一夜之間，在烏魯木齊消失了上萬人，不是被抓走就是被殺害。」

「中國政府發表：從翌朝在自治區挨家挨戶搜索，拘捕維吾爾的男人四千以上。」

當場的「人民日報」記者，最後，惡意的詢問：「妳在新疆是大富豪，卻說維吾爾人沒有自由。」她立即反問的說：「我們因不要受壓制而遭彈壓，我們夫婦及孩子都被抓而坐牢。若是真正的新聞記者必須是睜大眼睛，挖掘事實的真相，做真實的報導才對吧。」（著名日本政治評論家・櫻井よしこ——「週刊新潮」九月七日號）

卡提爾，亦去過澳大利亞，因為她的自傳作品「關於愛的十個條件」，被澳大利亞・墨爾本（Melbourne）的國際電影展覽會時提出特別演出。她在澳大利亞說：「維吾爾人，好似西藏人的兄弟，在國際社會老是不能發言。」

　　但是，以卡提爾作品被上演爲理由，中國政府卻從墨爾本國際電影展取消七個中國參展的作品。

　　奇怪的是，應該與中共政府無相干的「台灣」中華民國，也與中共政權同聲附和，將要展出的作品也一併退出電影展（日本・產業經濟新聞華盛頓支局長・山本秀也的報導）。後來，馬英九政權，更以「恐怖份子」爲由拒絕卡提爾來台灣，這無形中讓人看到中國共黨當局的政治力之大，及馬英九對中共的卑躬屈膝。

（六）維吾爾民族起義與台灣獨立運動的節操

　　此次目睹中國共黨政府手拿機關槍，帶著大砲坦克的武裝警察，對付一群手無寸鐵的維吾爾的抗議民眾，立即讓我想到台灣的二二八事件，當時也完全是由有武裝的軍隊、警察及特務，以機關槍、大砲來對付無武裝的台灣民眾，新疆這次的起義被彈壓、殺害，在台灣人看來儼然是二二八的翻版。

　　中共政權，以中華民族主義來恐怖統治所謂的中國少數民族，特別是圖博（西藏）民族和維吾爾民族。然而，這兩個被壓迫民族，百年來，不但沒有衰亡，也沒有失去其做人應有的志氣，更加地繼續不斷的在中國各地，以集體行動或單獨個人的犧牲性命，去對抗中共政府和中華民族的優越・差別和鴨霸的凌辱，實是令人敬佩！

　　反觀台灣，二二八時犧牲無可計數的台灣人的性命，不但在政治上、經濟上被壓迫、被掠奪，尚且台灣意識更被以恐怖洗腦的方式受到摧殘，台灣人在如此殘暴不堪的殖民地統治之下，二二八之後的台灣人卻僅以微小的抗議活動，或動嘴巴與國民黨謾罵，就自以為夠了，更有的在光天化日下與敵人妥協，有的或明或暗和中國共黨眉目傳情。當這些人曾高喊台灣獨立時，影響了多少的台灣大眾，台灣人受到他們的感召都挺身而出為台灣打拚，其後遭到這些台灣獨立號召者的敵前投降，台灣大眾又該要如何自處？

　　在面對維吾爾民族如火如荼的爭取獨立自主，台灣獨立運動民眾更應該以這次新疆事件為殷鑑，由歷史中學習祖先們不屈不撓的反抗外來政權的志氣，體認到唯有台灣實現獨立建國，才是台灣人唯一的活路。

第二部

故土台灣

3.
台灣民族主義

台灣民族主義是台灣史的產物，
身爲台灣人，咱應了解台灣的過去與未來

　　台灣民族主義，是唯一能救台灣人子子孫孫永世出頭天，幸福永世安居樂業在台灣的意識價值概念。台灣民族主義是台灣人共同力行遵守的信念。台灣民族主義，是台灣人大團結的一枝旗幟，促使台灣成爲眞正有公義的獨立國家。請細讀祖先們嘔心瀝血所留下的台灣民族主義的初步概念。

（一）認識台灣史的四大焦點

　（1）殖民地社會
　（2）本地反唐山、出頭天做主人的志氣
　（3）唐山人回中國、本地人成爲台灣人
　（4）台灣民族凝結、台灣民族主義崛起

　　台灣四百年有史以來，物質方面的社會建設眞發展，

移民・開拓・資本主義化・近代化等非常進步，結果，到一九三〇年代初，台灣在亞洲，已是次於日本的近代工業化地區。

不過，台灣在這四百年中，一貫是受外來侵略者的殖民統治，自己攏無做過主人，所以台灣長久以來都屬「殖民地社會」，這點就是台灣歷史的焦點之一。（什麼叫做殖民地社會？外來侵略者武力侵佔他人的領土、霸佔土地、統治剝削甲掠奪當地人，就是殖民統治。）

因爲這樣，所以台灣代代祖先攏起來做反對外來侵略者的殖民統治。

荷蘭統治時代，郭懷一漢人移民・原住民等攏起來做「反紅毛蕃仔」的反抗鬥爭。

滿清時代的殖民統治台灣很特殊，滿清政府派遣漢人的做官・做兵・大地主等來管台灣，這些漢人統治者（三、六年就調換回中國），卻繼承荷蘭時代的殖民體制來管被統治漢人的開拓農民，而且這些漢人統治者比在中國大陸時代都更苛刻，更無人道，雖然雙方攏是漢人，但在台灣卻分裂爲「本地人」甲「唐山人」的兩個陣營，因此在二百餘年間，本地農民大眾朱一貴・林爽文等連續的起來做了「本地反唐山」「三年小反五年大亂」的抗爭。如此雙方冤冤相報的做了激烈的武裝鬥爭的結果，被壓迫的本地人陣營遂產生了「本地人要出頭天做主人」的這種宿願甲志氣。這就是台灣的歷史焦點之二。本地人的這個宿願甲志氣一代傳過一代，而成爲本地人子孫的精神傳統。

　　一八九五年，滿清在甲午戰爭戰輸日本，台灣才再淪陷為日本帝國主義的殖民地。此時，在台灣的唐山人（舊統治者）攏總回歸中國大陸（一八九七年歸回中國大陸六、四五六人為最後一批），留在台灣的本地人攏被編入日本國籍，叫著台灣人。這就是台灣歷史的焦點之三。

　　日本統治時代，台灣資本主義發達，社會近代化進展，西洋文明傳入台灣，台灣人初等教育普及化，青少年的文化‧技術水準上升。

　　當在此時，世界潮流的「殖民地解放‧民族獨立」的思想甲運動傳入台灣，促使台灣人出頭天做主人的精神傳統發展為「抗日運動」。如林獻堂‧蔣渭水等的「台灣文化協會」「台灣議會設立運動」「台灣民眾黨」、簡吉等的「台灣農民組合」，謝雪紅的「台灣共產黨」、王詩琅等的「無政府主義派」，攏起來做激烈的抗日鬥爭，不但是當時的讀書人知識份子，一般台灣大眾也廣泛的參加抗日戰，流傳為「番薯仔反四腳」的抗日鬥爭，結果，台灣社會凝成近代概念的「台灣民族」，「台灣民族主義」崛起。這就是台灣歷史的焦點之四。

　　一九四五年第二次世界大戰終結後，蔣家國民黨中華民國在美軍的軍艦甲飛機掩護之下，即以：

　　（Ⅰ）以中華民族主義為理念

　　（Ⅱ）六十萬美式武裝的軍閥部隊

　　（Ⅲ）三十萬法西斯特務網甲警察系統

　　（Ⅳ）三十萬中國傳統封建官僚

來佔領台灣，同時劫收日本帝國留下的龐大的「殖民統治體制」甲其設施·物資等，以及四十萬日本軍裝備，而來做了殖民統治剝削及大屠殺。

此時，台灣人甲中國人，在社會範疇上，已經分爲「台灣民族」甲「中華民族」，中華民族主義成爲外來殖民統治者的理念，故台灣仍然呻吟於殖民統治體制之下。

一九四九年中國共產黨建立中華人民共和國，共產帝國主義現以龐大的陸海空軍甲一千四百餘枚飛彈，虎視眈眈的企圖侵攻台灣，鄧小平在一九八○年代，曾對台灣問題說過：「中國共產黨的理論基礎是共產主義，但我們更是中華民族主義。」

（二）台灣為什麼要獨立，
　　　獨立鬥爭的對象是誰？

台灣現在仍在中華民族外來侵略者殖民統治之下，所以我們台灣人必須逐行台灣獨立革命運動。

台灣人，繼承了出頭天做主人的歷史傳統，爲了自己做台灣的主人，同時也爲了要做甲世界的人能平起平坐的一個自由平等的人，必須爭取台灣民族獨立，建立獨立國家，才能保持自己的前途甲利益。

台灣·台灣人，爲了從殖民統治解放實現民族獨立，有兩種革命對象，即兩個敵人。一個是現正殖民統治台灣的中國國民黨中華民國，再一個是以龐大的武力將要侵攻台灣的

中國共產黨中華人民共和國。

中國國民黨甲中國共產黨要佔領並殖民統治台灣這一點，雙方的立場是一致的。中國國民黨現乃成爲妨害台灣獨立解放的看門狗，中國共產黨則成爲中國國民黨要永久殖民統治台灣的後台。

從台灣·台灣人來說，中國國民黨中華民國甲中國共產黨中華人民共和國，同樣是妨害台灣要實現獨立所得排除的兩個革命對象、兩個敵人。

（三）台灣民族主義概念

自古以來，凡有的民主革命·民族革命或殖民地解放運動，起碼要有理念·立場·戰略戰術的一系列基本概念，即有明確的理念·堅定的立場，及有效的戰略戰術，革命才能成功。這是世界上許多革命運動所顯示過的榜樣。

然而，很不可思議的，台灣獨立革命運動已做了快到六十年了，從來沒有聽到或者感觸到這種基本概念。這點不外是促使台灣獨立革命遲遲不進的很大原因。

這一系列的革命基礎理論，是透過深切知道客觀資料（歷史的·現在的），再加以理性或智慧的分析研究，結果，才學到五年、十年，或二十年……的革命運動發展規律的認識及革命實踐。這叫著「知性革命」（rational revolutionary movement）。

相反的，假若欠缺這種革命基本理論·基本道理，而

茫茫然的、無預測無方針無計劃的，僅憑一過性的衝動的革命運動，這叫做「感性革命」（revolutionary movement on emotion）。感性革命具有偶發性、缺乏革命的理論甲風格，往往會停滯於欺瞞甲虛言，先是謾罵敵方，而來自我陶醉，並墮落於自信過高、自傲自大的個人英雄主義。如果是這樣，不可能團結全體同胞而戰勝外來統治者。

（四）台灣民族主義內涵

台灣獨立革命的理念，是「台灣民族主義」。

「台灣民族主義」，是台灣的歷史產物。決心要為台灣的前途甲利益打拚，台灣獨立革命運動，假若沒有革命理念（Ideologie），連對台灣歷史的認識攏無清楚，也少有革命的實際行動的話，就不可能在革命鬥爭裡取勝。

台灣民族主義是台灣革命的理論原則，革命行動的準繩，成員團結‧組織的旗幟，及革命力量的泉源。

什麼是台灣民族主義？

> 台灣人關心台灣的前途甲利益，
> 政治上要建設台灣獨立國家，
> 經濟上要發展台灣國民經濟，
> 文化上要發展台灣固有文化的思想甲行動。

然而，從一九五〇、六〇年代，海外台灣獨立運動開始

以來，有些居留海外的獨立運動者，卻宣稱：「民族主義思想已經落伍了。」對於台灣歷史一知半解的這些少數台灣人的這種謬論，後來傳進台灣島內，竟使大家不能也不敢講出「台灣民族主義」這句名稱。

其實，落伍的並不是民族主義思想，而是那些台灣獨立運動者的腦筋，他們不但是自己落伍，竟使一般台灣人誤解民族主義的概念甲歷史意義，妨害了台灣獨立革命的前進。

且看第二次世界大戰結束後，亞洲・非洲及中南美洲的所有被壓迫民族（當時全世界的殖民地人口佔世界總人口的七○％），因以民族主義思想為基本理論甲行動的旗幟，而向帝國主義遂行鬥爭，結果到了一九六○年代，全世界的被壓迫民族幾乎攏達成民族獨立而建立自己的國家。現在，只有剩下擁有二千餘萬人口的台灣，甲人口三、五萬的十幾個島嶼，還在外來殖民統治體制之下，未有自己的國家。思想起來，凡在近代世界，民族主義思想是如此留下劃時代的歷史意義。

殖民統治台灣的中國國民黨中華民國，甲宣稱要用武力侵略台灣的中國共產黨中華人民共和國，攏正在大聲叫囂「中華民族主義」為殖民統治的理論指導。反而是被統治的台灣・台灣人還抬不起「台灣民族主義」的旗幟。

更糟糕的，近來台灣人（特別是知性主義的台灣知識階層），不但不敢談「獨立」甲「獨裁」等言辭，而以似是而非的「民主」或莫須有的「威權」這種抽象虛言來取代。自己不敢說獨立、不敢說台灣民族，誰能幫助獨立革命？

　　台灣‧台灣人，爲了戰勝外來殖民統治者，必須經常深化認識甲加強行使台灣革命理念的台灣民族主義。

獨立台灣會

24249　北縣新莊市中平路110巷17號3樓

電話：(02)2363-2366

傳眞：(02)8993-1053

http://www.tw400.org.tw

E-mail:subeng@ms24.hinet.net

4.
台灣獨立的歷史必然性[1]

　　這幾十年來，我一直在思考要怎麼做（怎麼辦）？因為若要推翻國民黨的殖民體制，實在是一個移山倒海的大工程。尤其是敵人力量大，咱的力量還小的時候，咱就必須從對現實的認識出發。

　　我想在座各位大部分是學理工的，所以在進入主題之前，我先提一下社會科學的研究方法，基本上社會科學的方法論是採取「歷史的」和「論理的」雙向並重的方式。譬如我們研究一個蘿蔔，就必須從兩個方向著手，縱的切下去，是看其成長過程，即歷史的；橫的切下去，是看其紋理結構，即論理的。人是社會的動物，有其歷史的發展，研究人的問題更應從這兩方向著手。

　　研究台灣的問題因此須從歷史的及論理的兩個面向，來分析我們所面對的現實。現實的因素有三項：第一是歷史，第二是社會構造，第三是大眾的願望（在古早封建時代，第三項是不存在的）。在歷史上，台灣在古早被視為只是海中一

---

1 台灣學生社91年夏令營專題演講，兩全整理。

塊沒有用的土堆，清朝的記載中即稱之「丸泥」。為什麼那時侯一個沒用的土堆，在四百年後卻發展成亞洲僅次於日本的工業「地區」呢？（我們因為沒國家，只能被稱做「地區」，這是很可悲的事情。）

　　換言之，這四百來台灣的社會已經形成了。社會的形成有兩個重要的基礎，一是物質基礎，一是精神基礎。台灣社會形成的物質基礎有移民的勞動力，赤腳的開墾，加上日本人的資本主義化和現代化；精神基礎方面，台灣人很慘，可以說是災難深重，四百年來，我們都是受外來者的統治。先是荷蘭人，繼而滿清、日本、及現在的國民黨集團。咱們的祖先開墾鄉土很打拚，而且做為一個「人」也相當有骨氣。荷蘭時代是叫做漢人反紅毛，滿清時代叫做本地人反唐山，日本時代則是台灣人反帝國主義（也叫做四腳仔），228時期及50年代則是番薯仔反阿山，60及70年代變成反芋仔。這些反抗最後都被鎮壓下去，並且犧牲了很多生命，流很多血。然而也塑造出咱的精神傳統，也就是「出頭天」。

　　反荷蘭人、反滿清、反日本人、反唐山，皆是在反抗外來的殖民統治，為著要出頭天自己做主。「出頭天」這句話本身即有相當的意義，我走遍中國大陸各地，從來沒聽過中國人說這句話（他們用的類似語為「翻身」）。所以說「出頭天」是咱的精神傳統，是用血和生命所換來寶貴的歷史傳統，也是咱台灣人的文化。這個精神傳統，咱若用現代政治學和社會學的放大鏡一照，就知道這個「出頭天」就是要獨立，要來建立自己的國家，也就是咱台灣人的民族主義

（Taiwanese Nationalism）。

　　台灣為什麼要獨立呢？大部份都會回答說因為國民黨殖民統治，獨裁沒民主，所以要獨立。這種說法並不是很正確，因為那有一天國民黨民主不獨裁了，台灣就不需要獨立了嗎？我的回答很簡單，只有一句話：「不一樣。」是什麼不一樣呢？番薯和芋仔就是不一樣。也許有人要問，我們的祖先也是從中國來的，為什麼說台灣人和中國人是不一樣呢？要解釋這個問題也很簡單，以近代民族學的觀點來看，我們在種族上和中國人是一樣（都是漢族），但是在民族上咱就和他們不一樣。剛才我提到，古早時候移民和大陸人都稱為漢人，到了清朝末年就變成本地人和唐山人，這就是民族形成的一個前提，也是未成熟的民族主義（pre-nationalism）。經過日本時代的資本主義化現代化，才名符其實地形成台灣民族和台灣民族主義。

　　十多年前，我在美國剛提出台灣民族主義時，很多知識份子都無法接受。台灣的教育水準雖高，知識份子都一肚子的學問，不過往往變成有「知識」沒「常識」。怎麼說是沒常識呢？試問：要國家（Nation）但是沒民族主義（Nationalism）如何能形成國家呢？這只是常識，但卻被大家忽略了。要建立一個Nation，可是卻沒有Nationalism做為理念上的基礎（backbone），如何來建立一個國家？！這是台灣四十多年來獨立運動最大的缺陷。所以我說目前咱台灣要獨立已備有「天時」與「地利」，但是「人和」還是欠缺。大家對台灣民族主義不瞭解，沒有用台灣民族主義做為

理念上統合的基礎，於是各說各話，往往不歡而散。好在這兩三年來，接受台灣民族主義的人愈來愈多，這是很好的事情。台灣要獨立是歷史的必然，台灣的歷史中已經有這個根，是咱祖先用血和生命灌溉而成的，這點我們必須去深刻體會。

我們來看孫文當年反抗滿清，也是有理念基礎，他的旗子就是「中國民族主義」。打完滿清後，他再提出「中華民族」的口號。當年國民黨來取台灣時，其就是拿著這面旗子（繡上「三民主義」）。今日中共在統戰台灣時，也是拿著這面旗子（不過繡上「共產主義」）。就連目前流亡在海外的所謂中國民主人士，如六四學運份子，都毫無例外地宣稱台灣是他們（中國）的。這是他們的大國主義（Great Nationalism）。所以說，三方會戰，他們兩個都有拿旗子，我們連一面旗子都沒有，是如何與人作戰呢？

現在我們接著來談第二個現實因素，台灣的社會構造。台灣的社會一直是受外來者管的殖民統治，這點大家必須要認清。何謂殖民統治呢？受外來者霸佔、掠奪和剝削的社會構造即是。但是有人會說，像國民黨集團也和我們同樣是漢族啊，為何說他們是外來者呢？這個理由很簡單，在台灣人四百年的血淚奮鬥史裡（在台灣民族的形成過程中），1945年以後才來佔領台灣的國民黨集團並沒有參與過，所以說他們是外來者。而且更重要的是，他們統治台灣人的方式在本質上和日本人、滿清、荷蘭人是沒什麼不一樣的。同時咱也要了解，咱要反的不是殖民的人（中國人），是要反殖民的體

制。

國民黨的殖民體制在本質上是一個封建的外來政權集團，包括有封建的軍閥及法西斯式的特務系統以及他們的幫兇，台灣人買辦（請參見我所製的圖表：圖一）。我再強調，

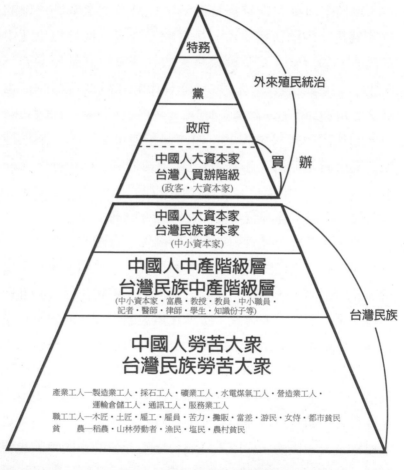

特務

黨

政府

外來殖民統治

中國人大資本家
台灣人買辦階級
（政客・大資本家）

買　辦

中國人大資本家
台灣民族資本家
（中小資本家）

中國人中產階級層
台灣民族中產階級層
（中小資本家・富農・教授・教員・中小職員・
記者・醫師・律師・學生・知識份子等）

台灣民族

中國人勞苦大眾
台灣民族勞苦大眾

產業工人─製造業工人・採石工人・礦業工人・水電煤氣工人・營造業工人・
　　　　運輸倉儲工人・通訊工人・服務業工人
職工工人─木匠・土匠・雇工・苦力・攤販・當差・游民・女侍・都市貧民
貧　　農─稻農・山林勞動者・漁民・塩民・農村貧民

圖一：台灣社會殖民統治構造

大家要認清楚統治者的本質，我們要打倒就是這種壓迫人的
「體制」，不是外來的「人」。像我所提到的「買辦」，在
經濟學上這是殖民統治的必然產物，外來者要來統治殖民地
時人地生疏，必須培養一些幫手。這些幫手替外來者剝削自
己的同胞，這就是「買辦」。國民黨的這種殖民本質是一直
不變，蔣經國死後，國民黨內一片混亂，不過他們很識時務
也很高招，立即抬出李登輝來收買台灣人的人心，尤其是中
產階級的台灣人對李登輝產生了極大幻想。連郝柏村都說現
在總統是台灣人在做，縣市長也有台灣人在做，你們台灣人
出頭天了。

　　其實，對台灣的歷史和社會沒有徹底了解的人，才會
對李登輝產生幻想。這種假象下階層的民眾反而看得比較清
楚。我在日本曾和台灣來的卡車司機開玩笑說：「恭喜啦！
你們台灣人出頭天啊！現在總統是台灣人在當了！」他苦笑
地回答我說：「你也別說笑，誰不知李登輝是番薯皮芋仔
肉！」所以說群眾的眼睛是雪亮的，下階層的人雖然不善於
講、不善於說，但原則性的東西卻看得很透澈。這個原則就
是在台灣雖然這些統治者在種族上是和我們一樣，但是在社
會構造上台灣還是殖民地，在這殖民地上有一些台灣人幫忙
著統治集團（或已變成其一部分）在剝削台灣人。

　　接著，我們來談第三個現實因素，群眾的願望。其實，
大家也都了解，要打倒國民黨，推翻其體制，非得靠群眾的
力量不可。在當時西方新興的資本家階級，為著打破封建的
束縛，因為本身仍然是少數者，也得去動員廣大的農奴群

眾，告之一旦封建主打倒後，你我大家都是自由平等，所以
才能打倒封建的體制。之後，民族才形成，小圈圈打破，大
圈圈圍起來。所以說，種族是利用血緣的相同結合起來；民
族卻是因為經濟利益和政治命運的相同結合起（大圈圈）。
民族的形成，英國是在十七世紀，法國是在十八世紀，德
國是在十九世紀。日本人看到這個「民族」（Nation）很厲
害，也將這個英文文字，翻譯成「國家」（這並不是中國人翻
譯的）。孫文當時在日本也體會著這個「民族」的厲害，於
是才提出「中國民族」的口號。

　　現在我們瞭解著，在立場上咱是殖民地的被統治者，國
民黨集團則是殖民地的統治者，我們的理念是祖先留下來的
台灣民族主義，接著我們應該「怎麼辦」呢？怎麼辦裡頭必
須有行動，要革命，才能推翻體制。革命有兩種方式，一種
是自然發生，另一種是現代的革命方式。自然發生就是人民
被壓迫到走投無路只好起而反抗，如清朝時代三年一小反、
五年一大反即是。二二八事件也是一樣，就是台灣人的意志
並沒結合，當中南部的青年學生和工人都還在拚命流血，
在台北的高級知識份子卻和中國人在談和，讓陳儀有機會爭
取時間，用緩兵之計，結果中國軍隊一到，台灣人被殺得很
慘。所以說不能採用「自然發生」的革命方式，咱應走「現
代革命」的方式。

　　什麼是現代的革命方式呢？四個要素必備：第一是理
念，第二是組織，第三是要有計劃，第四是聯合。這不是我
的發明，這是兩三百年來由階級鬥爭，民族解放鬥爭，以及

殖民地鬥爭所綜合出來的方法。理念是最高的指導方針，沒靈魂（geist, 德文）是無法和別人作戰。你們看民進黨雖然有人在喊獨立，但有人卻和國民黨在妥協，也有人跑去北京，在這種情形下，你叫群眾要跟誰？無理念的組織，就像失去桶箍的木桶，無法緊密地結合起來，可稱之為「幫派」，不是「組織」。咱的理念不用說就是台灣民族主義，有理念的革命才能成功，咱就是要用台灣民族主義來對抗壓迫咱的中華民族主義。

組織是非常地要緊。人類生存一直是power的問題，power有：有形力量和無形力量。有形力量馬上可以發揮作用，在台灣如政治、經濟、軍事和特務，這些有形的力量幾乎都在國民黨的手中，台灣人一點也沒有。至於無形的力量，咱台灣人很大很足（須有媒介來轉變成有形力量），國民黨卻是很小很弱。在政治上咱是受欺侮的，要和他們爭是光明磊落的事情，何況咱人也比他們多。但是沒組織就無法變成有形的力量，只是烏合之眾，可見組織的重要。然而要如何組織，台灣人其實並沒深刻的體會。組織最重要的是要民主，組織若是獨裁是不行的。組織有中央和支部，決策不能都在中央，必須到下面去討論，最後再交回中央綜合執行，這樣才是有血有肉的組織。這樣的組織才會有紀律，因為你我決議好的事情，大家就要遵守。

計劃也是非常地要緊，咱不能頭痛醫頭、腳痛醫腳，沒有計劃就會一天到晚任人擺佈，這樣一切都會變成白費。在計劃上，咱必須了解什麼是合乎台灣大環境的戰略、戰術，

這點還有待大家來加以研究。

最後咱談到「聯合」。聯合最重要是結合勞苦大眾、中產階級和民族資本家，凡是國民黨集團統治階層以外的都要聯合起來（參見圖一）。什麼是民族資本家？譬如那些只有十幾個員工的中小企業，或是沒和國民黨官商勾結的生意人。這些人咱都得聯合起來，這樣反對陣營才有夠大。這個想法進一步牽連著我的「兩段革命論」。以下略述（其實也跟咱的獨立建國相當有關連）。

台灣的資本主義並不是由自己的社會中發展出來的，是日本人為著要提高生產，加強剝削台灣，才將資本主義移入台灣。日本人在經濟上讓台灣資本主義化，政治上卻不民主化。當時台灣一半以上的財富由日本人拿去，剩下來才給廣大的勞動者和中小企業。這種的殖民體制，國民黨過來就順手接收起來，不但如此，國民黨還將「封建」的寶貝拿來套住台灣，抓住了台灣百分之七十以上的資源，所以說台灣的資本主義是「跛腳的資本主義」。

在這種的情形下，咱不能採用階級鬥爭的躍進方式，必須採取二階段的革命。首先聯合民族資本家，除去台灣矛盾的總根源：殖民地體制。也就是民族解放先來，建國先來。把資本主義正常化以後擴大生產，提高經濟力，社會民主化，那時候再進入社會主義革命（有可能就不須流血）。這就是「兩段革命論」，先是民族（打倒外來者）民主（建立民主社會）革命，達成後才可以進入社會主義的階段。

綜合來說，現代的革命方式必須是有理念的組織，加

上配合台灣大現實的計畫，並聯合台灣被壓迫及剝削的各
階層，這樣才能發揮力量。台灣獨立是歷史的必然，台灣人
關心台灣的前途和利益，在政治上要建立獨立自主的國家，
在經濟上要建設台灣的國民經濟，在文化上要發展固有的
台灣文化，在這個思想下再配合革命的行動，這就是台灣
民族主義。有了這個台灣民族主義（Taiwanese Nationalism）的
backbone，咱才能真正建立咱台灣人自己的國家（Nation）。

現場問答

【問】你剛才提到現在是台灣獨立的天時地利，請問「天
　　　時」指啥？

【答】天時就是現今國民黨日漸腐敗，中共亦是。中共一天
　　　到晚喊說他們要來打咱，其實他們的戰略沒別的，只
　　　有兩種：一種是武取，另一種是統戰。當他們用統
　　　戰，一天到晚大力叫喊，你就知道他們是無能力強用
　　　武取。

【問】目前台灣的運動漸漸有娛樂的取向（用輕鬆的方式來抗
　　　爭），這種方式是否有可能成功？若不行，是不是非
　　　採「革命」的方式不可？

【答】這個問題要從計劃上的戰略及戰術來說。戰略是根據
　　　理念和台灣的大現實，大現實包括人文、地理、敵我
　　　力量比較等。戰略的具體實現就是戰術，比如遊行時

路有多寬，路線該如何走，警力佈署有多少……，這些如何作戰的指導就是戰術。你指的就是戰術的問題。中產階級想要輕鬆的方式來打倒國民黨，行得通當然最好，但是這是不可能的。須知這個（台灣）殖民體制已經四百多年了，根深蒂固，須拚生死才有可能，光是唱歌遊街是無法爭取得什麼的。

【問】何謂「革命」？一般人聽到革命好像就是流血，你所提到的革命是啥麼？

【答】「革命」其實並不是可怕的東西。革命就好像「犁田」，譬如換朝代只是改政策，但換體制卻是犁田一般地從根拔除，然而前者卻可能比後者留更多的血（中國的歷史可查），所以革命並不是太恐怖的東西。革命是（1）理念、（2）組織、（3）武裝革命、（4）聯合、（5）民主鬥爭的綜合。咱不要光看英、美等國今日的民主成就，他們是經過很多人的犧牲，付出了很大的代價，用革命流血才換得他們的民主制度。誰也不願流血，割到小指頭我也會痛，但是一旦碰上了就無法逃避。這革命是不得已的，否則是無法推翻體制的。

【問】你說現在台灣不能用選舉，要用革命。是不是實行革命後，再來用選舉？

【答】不，我說選舉也需要。在島內運動的人，若不用選舉

的方式，直接就要革命，有如拿拳頭母去擊石獅。但是光用選舉是無法解決問題，必須要一方面參與體制內的選舉，另一方面進行體制外的革命運動。基本上，這是兩個戰略，但是路線卻一致，路線即要獨立。島內在運動開始時無法說「獨立」，只好喊「民主」，但往往走下去，工具（民主）卻變成目的，真正的目的（獨立）倒不見了。張俊宏年初到日本訪問，三大新聞之一的每日新聞問他選舉後民進黨要幹什麼，張則答說要和國民黨聯合政權。所以這種「只可以說不可以做」的民主，實在大有問題。一些知識份子走在群眾後面，選舉時用「獨立」應付一下，選舉後就忘了。至多，只是在國會議堂內扭扭打打。

【問】革命成功後，革命的力量如何運用才能達到民主制度？否則是不是又變成另一個獨裁政權？

【答】這個問題很要緊！原則上，組織一定要採取民主的方式。「民主集中制」並非蘇俄的專利，資本主義國家如英美的國會民主亦是經由民主方式之決策後集中執行。沒錯！選舉後民進黨可能換下國民黨，如果民進黨的內部不民主，仍然是換湯不換藥，也有獨裁的可能。所以在打倒外來政權的過程中，咱一定要強化下階層民眾的力量，如此才能達到真正的民主。權力是相當有魔力的。我也沒想到毛澤東在抗戰時顯得那麼民主，在取得政權之後卻變得那麼獨裁。

【問】社會主義和共產主義有什麼不同？

【答】其實馬克思對社會主義的藍圖也尚未規劃完全。一般
　　　來說，革命有（1）理論、（2）運動、（3）體制的
　　　三大階段。馬克思是由前兩者下手，列寧是直接從體
　　　制來，所以蘇俄的失敗是由列寧開始的。因為當時蘇
　　　俄是農民社會，資本主義尚未發達，列寧一下子就用
　　　社會主義做下去，社會不能接受，他就用獨裁。到史
　　　達林時，就往共產主義發展，更加獨裁，變成以官僚
　　　組織為基礎的個人獨裁，以致失敗。中國的失敗也是
　　　一樣，1949年取得政權後，1953年就進入社會主義，
　　　1958年人民公社，就進入共產主義，保證失敗。一般
　　　來說，社會主義是「各盡所能，各取所得」，共產主
　　　義是「各盡所能，各獲所需」。你們想這需要多大的
　　　生產力才能滿足呢？所以，我只說社會主義，從不說
　　　共產主義。說不定有一天社會主義實行後，會有比共
　　　產主義更好的東西發展出來呢！

　　　最後，我還有幾句話，也是對你們的一個建議。你們
現在最要緊的是要打定你們的人生觀。此去後，你們之中有
人去搞革命，有人去結婚生子，就沒機會再打定人生觀了。
賺大錢、大吃大喝也是人生觀。為了自己的利益，官商勾結
也能往上爬。革命只是你們一部份的人生觀，不是全部。我
知道學校的功課已經將你們弄得霧煞煞，自己的專門知識要
讀，但是有關哲學、歷史、文學、音樂、藝術都要去讀去接

觸，豐富你們的素養，擴寬你們的視野，找出人生最有價值
是做什麼事。經過這種思考，爲著「某某（代誌）」出力，
「某某」會進步，而得到自我的心安，這就是最高的人生
觀！

5.
認識歷史，以眞誠謙讓
的胸襟化解族群隔閡

　　每逢選舉，很必然的，就會看見族群問題被拿來大做文章，「族群大和解」、「激化族群對立」等名詞紛紛出籠。可是，經過一次又一次的選舉，並不見族群問題被嚴肅的討論過，族群問題似乎成了選舉專用名詞，選後就遺忘了，甚至有人乾脆說台灣不存在族群問題。但是，大家如果誠實一些，就必須承認台灣確實存在族群問題，當面對利益分配的時候，尤其難以迴避。而且，這個問題已經存在數百年，是台灣社會和諧以及獨立建國的一大障礙，是大家必須面對、解決的一個重大問題。

　　要解決問題，必須從瞭解著手，要瞭解台灣的族群問題，當然要從台灣的歷史切入。

　　台灣原本是原住民的居住地，四百年前，荷蘭人佔領台灣，漢人開始移民台灣以後，台灣社會的發展開始出現雛形。漢人移民台灣，在人地生疏的自然條件之下，為了求生存而自然的聚集在一起居住，這就形成了所謂的「角頭」。角頭的性質著重在對所居住的村莊的認同。（台灣一直都是由

外來者統治，不曾獨立建國，因此也沒有國家認同。）到了日據時代，開始引進資本主義，電話、鐵路等交通通訊設施使台灣全島得以貫通，因各地區交流暢通，原本以村莊爲中心的角頭認同擴大爲台灣整體的認同，與外來統治者相對立的「番薯仔」的概念於焉產生。

在番薯仔概念之下，其實還內含著族群的差異性，最主要的就是福客之間的差異。在漢人移民台灣的過程中，福建漳州、泉州的福佬人最先到來，潮州、汕頭、梅縣的客家人則比福佬人慢了一步，由於平原地區已經成爲福佬人的天下，這些遲到的客家人很自然的朝山坡地發展。因爲福佬人來得早，人數又多，逐漸產生了多數的橫霸，福客恩怨便因此開始。例如，明朝末年，福建南安人鄭芝龍以海賊爲業，因與潮州、汕頭客家區的海賊有仇，雙方便多所對立。到了清朝，施琅攻下台灣以後，頒佈「渡海三禁」：（1）想渡海來台者，必須先在原籍地申請「照單」（渡台証照）。（2）渡台者一律不准攜帶家眷。（3）粵地向爲海賊窟，不准其民渡台。第三條明令禁止客家人來台，這一道禁令也導致客家人移民台灣中斷長達一百多年。

台灣的族群對立，起先其實是一種最原始的求生存的戰爭。因爲福佬人的人數多，佔盡優勢，客家人便與外來者聯手對付福佬人，例如朱一貴之亂，客家人便與清廷聯手平亂。除了福客之爭，福佬人內部又有漳泉對立，就是所謂的分類械鬥。例如，林爽文是漳州人，鹿港則是以泉州人爲主的聚落，在林爽文之亂中，鹿港人便與清廷聯手平亂。此

外，台灣人內部還有角頭與角頭之間的對立，漢人與原住民之間的對立。後來，統治者為了更有效的統治，更刻意加以分化，加強各種對立關係，族群恩怨也因此而更為深化。

到了日本時代，福佬族群內部的分類械鬥因為彼此往來密切而趨於消弭，但是，與客家人之間的流通，則因為地域、語言、經濟形態的差異性導致接觸機會較少，因此福客恩怨缺少化解的管道與機會。國民黨佔領台灣之後，又刻意分化福客關係，更加深了福客之間的對立。

一直到現在，台灣的農業縣份仍然以客家人為主，而比較都市化、商業化的都市，則是以福佬人居多。因為經濟、語言、地域的不同，加上情緒化的挑撥，進一步產生政治上的對立現象。

其實，從日據時代開始產生番薯仔觀念之後，長期的風土文化發展，台灣早已經台灣民族化，無論是日本人或是國民黨的壓迫，都是針對台灣人全體，並不會分福佬人、客家人或是原住民。從歷史上了解台灣內部族群之間的恩怨與心結之後，大家應該有所覺醒，應該以更寬容謙讓的心互相對待。大家應該了解，長期生活在台灣島上的人都屬於台灣民族，構成一個命運共同體，而台灣獨立則是台灣人生存的唯一道路。台灣內部各族群之間政治生活上的隔閡，如果不能化解，必定是台灣獨立的一大障礙。為了化解這個障礙，台灣內部族群必須先和解。

和解不能光是嘴上說說，必須在政治、經濟等實質問題上力求平等。在歷史上，人數佔大多數的福佬人，已經長期

佔盡優勢，現在，福佬人必須以謙讓的心扶助其他弱勢族群達到平等。目前台灣人口比例上，客家人佔百分之十三，大陸人佔百分之十二，原住民約有四十萬人，其餘為福佬人。因此，在政治上，應該分上議院與下議院，下議院依照民主原則，一人一票選出國會議員，上議院則應該依照族群比例，在台灣人口多達四分之三的福佬人，絕對不可以拿百分之六十五以上的席次。因為修憲需要三分之二以上同意，因此，至少百分之三十五以上的席次必須由其他族群分配，才不會形成福佬族群獨裁危機。

　　也許有人會說，由於各族群通婚的結果，台灣住民早已族群融合，許多只會說福佬話的人，最近才發現自己的祖先原來是客家人或是平埔族人，因此，各族群人口比例未必如上述的估算。在這種情況下，要如何確認族群人數呢？其實，族群除了血統之外，也是一種認同。目前，多數台灣人的問題是不瞭解自己祖先的歷史，如果台灣要進行一次族群總普查，經由自由意志登記自己所屬族群，那麼，大家勢必要從祖譜著手。瞭解自己祖先的歷史，也就瞭解了台灣的歷史。當台灣人都瞭解了台灣史，才能建立清晰的台灣認同概念，所有的歷史恩怨才有了化解的頭緒。因此，要談族群和解，先探索台灣歷史吧！

【附錄一】

荒漠中的行者
A Giant in the Desert

作者：葉治平（Chih-Ping Yeh）

譯者：侯平文（Ping-Wen Hou）

自學生時代，我就是史明先生的「崇拜者」。他每到美國巡迴演講，總會到我家住一個禮拜左右。一方面小作休息，另一方面努力地向我「傳道，解惑」。雖然，充滿著小資產階級軟弱性格的我，終究是看不破「大是大非」，而未能追隨他走向「勞苦大眾」。但與史明先生的認識，的確改變了我對人生的許多看法。

At graduate school, I became a "worshiper" of Mr. Su Beng. Whenever Mr. Su Beng came to the US to lecture, he would stay at my place for a week or so. He would have some rest and then I would listen to his enlightening teachings. At the time, I more or less had a bourgeois mentality. I still do, albeit to a lesser degree. Never a model follower of Mr. Su Beng, he nonetheless helped me better understand the philosophy of socialism. Indeed, thanks to him, I changed my perspectives about life.

　　史明先生來美國演講，隨身衣物十分簡單，但隨機運送的卻總是兩大袋沈重的書籍和刊物。當時的演講者都已用投影機來顯示圖表，但史明先生卻還是用老式的手繪掛圖。每到各地演講，他都帶著一支長軸捲筒，裏面放著兩卷掛圖，一卷講「社會主義」，一卷講「台灣民族」。每次到機場接他，總看到他把長長的捲筒斜背在背後，像是一把三八步槍。他的身材高挺，留著一頭蓋頸的灰髮，而且總是穿著一套褪色的牛仔裝。這個模樣，總讓我聯想起70年代的「功夫」影集中，那背著長笛，走過沙漠的甘貴成。

　　Mr. Su Beng always travelled light, other than bringing with him two big bags of books and periodicals. Slide projectors used in lectures had become popular at that time. Yet, Mr. Su Beng still used the old fashioned hand-written posters. Everywhere he went, he carried a long "tube" for his two posters, one on socialism, the other on Taiwanese Nationalism. Each time I went to the airport to pick him up, he would invariably place these two tubes on his back, as if he were bearing a carbine. Mr. Su Beng was tall with a headful of grayhair. Clad in coarse and worn out blue jeans, he looked just like a 1970's "Kung-Fu" movie star carrying a flute walking through the desert.

　　攜帶一大堆書籍和掛圖搭飛機，使他感到十分不便。為了要增加自己的「行動力」，年逾七十的史明開始學習開

車，並考過了美國駕照。1988年夏天，他買了一輛七百元的
舊車，從加州開到紐約，參加美東夏令會，再到華府，然後
開到休士頓。當他來到達拉斯找我時，已經將近勞工節了。
小住幾天後，他又匆匆地趕著上路。道別後，他開始發動車
子。但那輛早該報廢的老爺車，繞過美國一大圈後，實在已
經力不從心。當史明花了十分鐘終於把車發動起來時，整條
街都已充滿了濃濃的汽油味。我想，他的年事已高，英文又
不很通，開著這樣的「銅罐仔車」要越過炎熱的東德州和亞
利桑那，實在有些冒險。所以勸他開我的車子走，但他堅持
不肯，還是駕著那輛老爺車，蹣跚地駛上了二十號公路。

Air travel with two big bags of books and
posters was very burdensome. Also, to improve his
mobility, Mr. Su Beng, at age over 70, started to learn
driving and passed the driving license test. In 1988,
he spent $700 for a used car. He drove from California
to New York to attend the Taiwanese-American
Summer Camp. Then, he went on to Washington,
D.C. and Houston. When he finally reached Dallas,
where I lived then, it was close to Labor Day. He
stayed for a few days and insisted on going on his
trip. Mr. Su Beng had a difficult time starting the car,
which, having run every corner of the country, was
beat up. After 10 minutes or so, he finally got the
car started; the exhaust fumes covered the entire
street. As Mr. Su Beng was old and his English was
not that fluent, I felt that driving a used car going

through east Texas and Arizona, where the weather was withering hot, was quite a dangerous adventure. I asked him to take my car if he must go. Mr. Su Beng refused. He took his used car and went on Interstate 20.

那天晚上，我接到了史明的電話。原來，他在公路邊一個偏僻的加油站停下來後，車子就發不動了。加油站設有修車場，但已經打烊，必須等到第二天才能修理，所以他決定在車裡睡一晚，要我不必擔心。第二天中午，他又打電話來告知，車子必須修理引擎，但那天是周末，接著又是勞工節，所以可能要等到禮拜二才能完成。加油站的人告訴他，最近的汽車旅館是在六十英哩外，所以他決定要在車子裡再「ㄍㄨ」幾晚。離開達拉斯時，我太太為他準備了一罐泡菜和一包饅頭，也就當做乾糧打點。我告訴他千萬不可，並想辦法要接他回來，但他婉拒，而且笑著說，比起當年偷渡日本的香蕉船，他這部「汽車旅館」算是「上等房」了。

That evening, I received Mr. Su Beng's telephone call. As I had feared, he had stopped at a gas station and the car would not start again. That gas station had repair shop, but it was late. He was told the earliest repair would not be done until the following day. He decided to sleep in the car for the night and told me not to worry about him. Next day around noon time, Mr. Su Beng gave me another ring. He said, the engine needed to be fixed. Alas, it was an weekend and the following Monday was Labor Day! Thus, he had to wait until Tuesday. The worker at the gas station told him that the nearest motel was 60 miles away. Mr. Su Meng then decided he would stay in his car for a few more days. Right before Mr. Su Beng left Dallas, my wife gave him a jar of preserved vegetable and a package of "steam bun." He said that it was enough for him for days. Worrying about him, I offered to come to his "rescue". Mr. Su Beng refused. He laughingly told me that, compared to taking a banana ship to sneak out of Taiwan to Japan, his own "motel" was "first-rate."

禮拜二，修車場告訴他，車子的引擎已經完全報銷，必須要到艾爾帕索市去買個新的，可能要等兩三天。但幾天後，車場老闆又告訴他，這種老車的引擎早已不再製造，所以要想辦法到附近的城市的廢車場去找個舊引擎來換。就這樣，一天又一天，在德州邊境的公路旁，七十歲的史明先生在他的「汽車旅館」裡「ㄍㄨ」了兩個多禮拜。在這期間，我們每天以電話聯絡。他告訴我，車廠的人對他很好，晚上也有公路警察來和他聊天。他每天早上幫車廠掃地，車廠也讓他在洗手間裡洗澡。我問他如何打發其他的時間，他愉快的回答，這段意外的「休假」讓他有時間把馬克思的《資本論》再從頭讀過一遍。

Tuesday, the repair shop broke bad news to him - the engine was totaled. He could go to El Paso, Texas to get a brand new engine but that would take two or three days. A few days later, the owner informed him that the engine for that model of car had been discontinued, but he was willing to look around for a used one. Day after day, the 70 year-old Mr. Su Beng stayed in his "motel" on the road side somewhere in Texas for more than two weeks. He told me that people in the repair shop treated him very nicely and the traffic patrolmen came over to chat with him at night. He helped clean the repair shop in the morning and used the restroom at the repair shop for baths. I asked him how he spent his spare time. He cheerfully replied: I used this rarely found "vacation" to re-read Karl Marx's *Das Kapital*.

　　車子終於修好了，大家都很高興。據說，那個引擎最後是在鳳凰城找到的。車廠的老闆對這個奇特的東方老人，不但好奇，也有好感。所以特別請他到家中吃了一頓牛排晚餐，以茲慶祝。史明先生也問我，將來可以從日本寄什麼禮物給車廠的人。我說，要送給德州佬，除了海帶，紫菜和魷魚絲之外，大概什麼都可以。問他這次「落難」有什麼感想，他說這個經驗使他更有信心，覺得自己還有體力和能力可以繼續「作運動」。此外，和車廠的工人相處，也使他瞭解到，美國不會發生工人革命。

Finally the car was fixed. Everybody was happy. The repair shop located an engine in Phoenix, Arizona. The owner of the repair shop expressed interest and admiration for the "strange old man from the Orient." He invited Mr. Su Beng home for a steak dinner to celebrate their achievement. Mr. Su Beng asked me what to send them as gifts when he returned to Japan. I said, for the Texans, just avoid those 'typical' Japanese delicacies such Nori (edible seaweed) or preserved squid, almost anything is fine. I asked him what he thought of this episode. He told me that the experience made him more self confident on his physique and his ability to continue to contribute to the Taiwan Independence Movement. Besides, after mingling with workers in the repair shop, he came to believe that there would be no such thing as the "workers' revolt" in the US.

　　每次想到史明先生，我總會憶起這多年前的往事。二十年來，台灣社會的變化很大，獨立運動也隨之起伏。過去所抱持的信念與原則，被稱爲「基本教義」；高喊「革命」的人則在體制內外進進出出。在這一片急功近利，翻雲覆雨的吵雜聲中，每聽到史明先生堅定，清晰，而且始終如一的言論，總使我聯想起，在那炎熱潮濕而且蚊蟲肆虐的荒漠中，史明先生平心靜氣地坐在破車裡研讀《資本論》的情景。記得，修車廠的老板曾在電話中問我，這個老人是不是某種宗教的修行者？我笑著回答，這個老人是個道地的無神論者，不過他確實是一個在奉行信念的實踐者。

　　Each time I think of Mr. Su Beng, I cannot help

but think of this incident.　For the last twenty some years, many changes have taken place in Taiwan and the Taiwan independence movement has waxed and waned accordingly.　The principles and ideals that all activists in the movement used to hold as "basic truths" are now being labeled as "fundamentalism", and those who are advocating "outside-of-system revolution" are flip-flopping driven by political power.　Whenever I hear Mr. Su Beng's clear and consistent teachings, I think of the old man in that hot and insect-infected desert calmly yet bravely reading Marx's *Das Kapital*.　I still remember the owner of the car repair shop asking me over the phone if the old man belonged to some kind of cult.　I answered with a laughter: "This old man is a true atheist, but is fulfilling what he truly believes in."

〔作者爲北美洲台灣人教授協會第二十三屆會長〕

【附錄二】

史明年表

1918年	出生於台北市士林施家，本名施朝暉，就讀台北市建成小學，並入台北一中（五年後留學日本）。
1942年	由日本早稻田大學政治經濟系的政治科畢業，旋至中國上海，參加中共陣營抗日。
1949年	五月因對中共徹底失望，而突破封鎖返回台灣。
1950年	二月集合二二八時倖免於難的三、四十名青年，在台北雙溪、苗栗大湖等地組織「台灣獨立革命武裝隊」。
1951年底	槍枝被國民黨發現，遂遭通緝。
1952年	三月逃至基隆，擔任港口搬運香蕉工人；五月搭貨輪天山丸潛赴日本，登陸時遭日本政府逮捕，後獲政治庇護。
1962年	「台灣人四百年史」日文版問世，改名史明。
1967年	主導成立「台灣獨立連合會」，旋因無法團結在日台獨運動而解散。同時，創立「獨立台灣會」。
1980年	「台灣人四百年史」漢文版發行。
1986年	「台灣人四百年史」英文版發行。
1993年	潛返台灣，於台南縣新營市高速公路被捕。
1994年	於高雄、台北、新竹、嘉義、台中、台東等地設立「台灣獨立宣揚車隊」，努力不懈致力台灣獨立革命行動。

1996年	成立「台灣大衆地下電台」（已於99年停播）。
2001年	設立「財團法人史明教育基金會」。
2005年	爲對抗中共提出「反分裂法」，集合各大學生於台灣大學門口靜坐一個月。
2005年 4月26日	爲因應中國國民黨連戰要去中國出賣台灣，獨立台灣會動員百輛計程車隊於高速公路上擋連戰，被法院判刑八個月，目前仍未結案。
2009年	與蔡丁貴「公投護台灣聯盟」舉辦「不爽，出來行」，由恆春行腳至台北市，共計五〇五公里。

有感於二十一世紀後的國際情勢瞬息萬變，但台灣人仍在中國國民黨外來殖民體制的統治下，過著紙醉金迷的日子，深感憂心忡忡，爲達到台灣民族解放的目標，至今仍奮戰不懈。

國家圖書館出版品預行編目資料

穿越紅色浪潮：史明的中國革命歷程與台灣獨
立之路 / 史明著. - - 初版. - - 台北市：台灣
教授協會出版：紅螞蟻總經銷，2010.03
168面：15×21公分

ISBN 978-986-81199-2-5（平裝）

1. 革命　　　　2. 民族獨立運動
3. 台灣獨立運動　4. 中國

571.71　　　　　　　　　　　　99003908

穿越紅色浪潮：
史明的中國革命歷程與台灣獨立之路

著　　　者　史　明
責 任 編 輯　周俊男
美 術 編 輯　宸遠彩藝
出 版 者　台灣教授協會
　　　　　　台北市臨沂街25巷15號1樓
　　　　　　Tel：02-2394-8797　Fax：02-2394-8798
　　　　　　http://www.taup.net
製 作 發 行　前衛出版社
　　　　　　10468 台北市中山區農安街153號4F之3
　　　　　　Tel：02-2586-5708　Fax：02-2586-3758
　　　　　　郵撥帳號：05625551
　　　　　　e-mail：a4791@ms15.hinet.net
　　　　　　http://www.avanguard.com.tw
總 經 銷　紅螞蟻圖書有限公司
　　　　　　台北市內湖區舊宗路二段121巷19號
　　　　　　Tel：02-2795-3656　Fax：02-2795-4100
出 版 日 期　2010年03月初版一刷
　　　　　　2019年10月初版二刷
定　　　價　新台幣200元